SECRETS TO SMOKING

ON THE WEBER SMOKEY MOUNTAIN COOKER *and* OTHER SMOKERS

AN INDEPENDENT GUIDE *with* MASTER RECIPES FROM A BBQ CHAMPION

BILL GILLESPIE

PITMASTER OF THE SMOKIN' HOGGZ BBQ,
ONE OF THE MOST DECORATED TEAMS IN THE COUNTRY

with TIM O'KEEFE

PAGE STREET
PUBLISHING CO.

PAGE STREET
PUBLISHING CO.

Copyright © 2015 Bill Gillespie

First published in 2015 by
Page Street Publishing Co.
27 Congress Street, Suite 103
Salem, MA 01970
www.pagestreetpublishing.com

Distributed by Macmillan; sales in Canada by The Canadian Manda Group.

19 18 17 16   7

ISBN-13: 978-1-62414-099-0
ISBN-10: 1-62414-099-8

Library of Congress Control Number: 2014940718

Cover and book design by Page Street Publishing Co.
Photography by Ken Goodman

Printed and bound in China

Page Street is proud to be a member of 1% for the Planet. Members donate one percent of their sales to
one or more of the over 1,500 environmental and sustainability charities across the globe who participate
in this program.

TO MY WIFE, SHAUNE

From the very beginning you believed in me, you have supported me in everything I do,
given me encouragement when I fail and have had this ability to always keep me thinking positive.
For this, I dedicate my first book to you in appreciation of everything you do for me.
You are my rock!!!! I love you.

GRAND CHAMPION
23RD ANNUAL
JACK DANIEL'S®
WORLD CHAMPIONSHIP INVITATIONAL BARBECUE
Lynchburg, Tennessee
October 22, 2011

CONTENTS

★ INTRODUCTION ★

If this book caught your attention, then chances are you're a barbecue enthusiast who wants to learn more about backyard cooking. When it comes to backyard cooking, the Weber Smokey Mountain Cooker (WSM) is among the best bang-for-your-buck cookers in today's world of barbecue. It is fairly simple to use, and you can obtain incredible results right away. With some knowledge and a little practice, you'll learn how to cook authentic barbecue reliably and repeatedly. Sound good? Great, because I am going to help you become a real pro at using the WSM!

What makes me think I can help you become a pro? Well, since 2008, my team Smokin' Hoggz has been active on the competition barbecue circuit. Initially, we had some good days, but we also had a few bad ones. Due to our willingness to learn from past mistakes, we got better at what we did, and things eventually became second nature to us. In fact, we were able to obtain high-quality cooking results time and time again. In 2011, our cooking techniques fueled a winning streak that we rode all the way to the Jack Daniel's World Championship—the most prestigious title in competition barbecue!

Shaune, Alan and I are not chefs by training or profession, and we like to think of ourselves as just regular people who love to cook in the backyard. We got started in competition barbecue cooking on a WSM, and now we're going to share a lot of the tips, tricks and techniques we've learned along the way. If we could learn to cook great food on the WSM, then we think you can too!

The Weber Smokey Mountain Cooker is one of the most versatile outdoor cookers on the market today. Its price point makes it accessible to most backyard enthusiasts, and its versatility makes it an outstanding value for the money. This single piece of cooking equipment allows you to use various backyard-cooking methods, including low and slow, hot and fast, a combination of both and standard grilling. This book contains 100 recipes to help you become familiar with every aspect of cooking on the WSM. Pretty soon you'll be tweaking these recipes to your own liking, and believe us, it won't be long before you're creating entire recipes on your own. Are you ready to get started?

➳ **We recommend keeping a cooking logbook. Any standard notebook will do. The important thing is to notate overall weather conditions, temperature, length of cook time, any tweaks you made to the recipe or cooking process and the end results of the finished product. Maintaining such a log will help you become a better cook, who can more accurately estimate how long it will take to complete the recipes you create.**

A FEW WORDS ABOUT TRADITIONAL BARBECUE

The world of barbecue sure is an interesting place. You could even say that it has its own unique culture. Unsurprisingly, barbecue culture contains oral history, lore, lots of sayings and various traditions. While the history of barbecue frequently sparks debate, something that is almost universally agreed upon is a basic definition. And that basic definition describes barbecue as using wood or charcoal to cook meat over a low-heat source for a long period of time. This definition gives rise to the expression "low and slow."

Another common agreement in barbecue pertains to the basic flavor profile. In traditional barbecue, the basic flavor profile consists of a spice rub applied to the meat prior to cooking, a smoke flavor that slowly seeps into the meat during the long cook time and a sauce that is layered on the meat during the final stages of the cooking process.

Well, that's pretty much where the agreements end. If you don't already know, then you'll quickly learn that the world of barbecue seems to have more debates than agreements. Take sauce, for instance. While sauce typically comprises part of the basic flavor profile, some regions of the country don't use sauce. Yet, even among the regions that do use sauce, you won't find continuity of flavor. Sauce preference in the flavor profile tends to be regional. Some regions prefer a sweet, sticky sauce, while other regions serve a hot, peppery sauce and there are also places that savor a pungent, vinegar-based sauce. Most regions claim that what they serve is the real version of barbecue. With all the debate about who is right and which way is best, discussing barbecue can become as heated as some Thanksgiving family gatherings. Fun, eh? Welcome to the world of barbecue!

SMOKE WOODS, CHIPS AND CHUNKS

In traditional barbecue, a primary component of the basic flavor profile is wood smoke. In essence, wood smoke is just another cooking ingredient that adds flavor to the meat. If you use too much smoke, the food can taste bitter. Yet, if you use too little, the food may be missing just a little something and fall flat. In addition to learning how much wood smoke to use while cooking, you'll also need to learn how to pair different types of wood with various meats and seafood.

Don't worry too much though, because we won't make you conduct extensive experimentation in order to determine which wood goes with what meat. Here is a basic list of the characteristics and uses for different woods that are commonplace on the competition circuit. Remember: Your personal preferences should always be the primary factor in determining the wood that you use.

WOOD	DESCRIPTION
Alder	Alder is a mild wood from the Pacific Northwest that's good to use with seafood, poultry, pork and light meat game.
Sugar Maple	Frequently found in the Northeast and a staple on the competition scene. It's smoky and mellow. Try mixing with one or two pieces of fruitwood for interesting flavor combinations. Works well with poultry, pork and cheese.
Hickory	Hickory is a popular wood that lends a hint of bacon flavor to the food you are cooking. Goes well with pork, ham and beef.
Mesquite	Mesquite is traditionally associated with Texas barbecue. Works well with beef. Use a little at first, as mesquite can overwhelm other flavors.
Apple	Mild, subtle, fruit flavor. Perhaps the most common of the fruitwoods, apple lends itself well to pork and chicken.
Peach	Think of this fruitwood as a milder version of hickory. Great with white and pink meats.
Cherry	Cherry wood creates a sweet-tasting smoke flavor that is great with pork and poultry. Cherry wood also lends a great color to pork butt or pork shoulder.
Walnut	This is a heavy flavor that lends itself to beef more so than pork or poultry. Walnut can be bitter if used alone, and is best used with some fruitwood.
Pecan	All around good wood for smoking. It has a sweet and mild flavor that is similar to hickory.

➽➤ **Smoke wood quickly sparks another debate, giving rise to yet more barbecue lore. We recommend soaking chips for about one hour, as it helps prevent them from quickly burning. Chunks are usually large enough that soaking them doesn't make much of a difference. When it comes to smoke wood, you'll hear that some people use fresh, green-cut wood, and other people use seasoned wood. Furthermore, there is debate about size: chunks or chips. And if that's not enough, more debate swirls around the notion of soaking smoke wood before adding it to the fire.**

TYPES OF CHARCOAL

The WSM cooks using convection, and the fire resides at the bottom of the cooker. Heat rises, filling the cooking chamber, and the unique design of the product's lid helps deflect heat back inward, toward the cooking grates. When cooking on the WSM, you have two primary types of charcoal to choose from as your fuel source for the fire: lump charcoal or charcoal briquettes.

In some ways, these fuel sources are similar. After all, briquettes are essentially made from lump charcoal; however, they contain binding agents (fancy terminology for chemicals) that help hold them together and retain their square shape. You might hear some people say that you should always light charcoal briquettes and let them turn grey before you use them to cook. Some people believe that this practice helps burn off some of the binding agents. Similarly, you might also hear some people say that if you place unlit, black charcoal briquettes directly on the fire and cook, the food will obtain a slight chemical flavor. This too is a reference to the binding agents. Some brands of briquettes use alternative binding agents, such as cornstarch, and label the product as natural briquettes. We prefer the natural briquettes, but you should try different brands to see what you like best.

People often refer to lump charcoal as being more natural than briquettes because lump charcoal contains no binding agents. Lump charcoal burns at a hotter temperature than briquettes, but it usually burns for a slightly shorter duration. If you want to get a long burn time for low and slow style cooking using lump charcoal, try closing the air vents at the bottom of the smoker. Closing the vents helps reduce the amount of oxygen that reaches the hot charcoal, slowing down the burn rate.

Some people prefer to cook using the same type of charcoal each and every time. This practice might enable you to better predict how long your food will need to cook. Other people prefer to change the fuel source depending on what food they're cooking. This might be a better option for more experienced cooks who are already familiar with various cook times on the WSM. Developing this level of familiarity was part of the fun for us!

➤➤ **Our preferred method is to drizzle some cooking oil on some newspaper before lighting it. The cooking oil prolongs the burn time of the newspaper, ensuring the charcoal is lit. We think the easiest way is to use a Weber Charcoal Chimney. There are a number of ways you can choose to light charcoal. We've seen people use things ranging from fire starter cubes to a blowtorch and everything in between. Using a charcoal chimney, you can set the charcoal ablaze by placing a crumpled up piece of newspaper at the base of the chimney and lighting it. One thing we absolutely DO NOT recommend using is charcoal lighter fluid. Lighter fluid is a chemical. Even after the fluid burns off, the chemical residue left behind will leave an unpleasant flavor lingering in the food.**

OVERVIEW OF THE WSM

The WSM is comprised of three primary sections: the base, the middle and the lid. Each section is porcelain-enameled, which makes the cooker easier to clean, highly resistant to corrosion and it retains heat well.

The base of the WSM contains a charcoal ring that houses lit charcoal. It also has three vents that control airflow. The amount of oxygen that reaches the hot coals directly influences the overall cooking temperature of the cooker.

The middle section contains two cooking grates and a water pan. The purpose of the water pan is twofold. First, the water pan produces steam, which helps prevent the food you are cooking from becoming dry. Second, after the internal temperature of the WSM stabilizes, the water pan helps regulate and maintain a constant temperature.

The lid contains one air vent. This vent typically remains open, and is crucial for sustaining the hot charcoal and channeling smoke through the cooker.

➤➤ **The WSM is available in three different sizes: 14.5 inch (37 centimeter) diameter for a total cooking area of 286 square inches (1844 square centimeters), 18.5 inch (47 centimeter) diameter (481 square inch [3102 square centimeters] cooking area), and 22.5 inch (57 centimeter) diameter (726 square inch [4682 square centimeters] cooking area). All of the recipes in this book were created using the 18.5 inch (47 centimeter) model. Slight changes pertaining to the amount of charcoal or cook times may be necessary if you are cooking on products of a different size.**

BASIC WORKFLOW AND OPERATING PROCEDURE

The versatility of the WSM may make it seem like a complicated piece of cooking equipment, but in reality, it's fairly simple to use—once you learn the basics, that is. After cooking on the WSM a few times, the basic workflow for setting it up and getting it going will become a regular routine, no big deal. To help get you started, we've outlined the basic workflow. Remember: When your WSM is not in use, you should always store it fully assembled and covered with a plastic drop cloth to help protect it from the elements.

➤➤ **SEASONING THE WSM: Before cooking on your new WSM for the first time, you should burn a batch of charcoal to help season it. Seasoning helps remove residue left over from the manufacturing process, such as trace amounts of dust, powder or oil. Seasoning also helps cure the paint, remove chemical odors and promote rust prevention. Additionally, you should clean the cooker every three or four times you cook on it. Clean the interior of the lid after every cook—otherwise, particles of soot can flake off and fall into your food.**

(continued)

BASIC WORKFLOW AND OPERATING PROCEDURE (CONTINUED)

1. Place the WSM on a flat surface.

2. Remove the top and middle sections from the base of the WSM, and set them aside.

3. Place the charcoal grate in the base of the cooker. DO NOT place the charcoal ring in the base at this time.

4. Place a charcoal chimney on the charcoal grate and fill it with charcoal.

5. Light the charcoal, and then wait for the coals at the top of the chimney to begin to turn gray.

6. When the coals at the top of the chimney begin to turn gray, use a pair of heat gloves to remove the chimney from the charcoal grate.

7. Place the charcoal ring in the base of the WSM.

8. Add about one-and-a-half chimneys of unlit charcoal. The amount of charcoal you add depends on how long you plan to cook. Ideally, you want to add enough charcoal now so that you can finish cooking without the need to add any additional charcoal later.

9. Carefully dump the hot charcoal on top of the unlit charcoal in the charcoal ring.

10. Place the middle section of the WSM on top of the lower section. Spray the cooking grates with nonstick cooking spray, and then place the grates into the WSM.

11. Place the water pan inside the middle section of the WSM.

12. Fill the water pan with warm or hot water.

13. Fully open all bottom vents.

14. Place the lid on the smoker. Leave the top vent open, and wait for the cooker to reach the temperature specified by the recipe you are using.

15. About 10 to 15 minutes before putting the meat on, open the side access door, and place some smoke wood on top of the hot charcoal. I use anywhere from one to five chunks of wood, depending on the recipe I'm using. I'm a New Englander, and I use what's local. For me, that's often sugar maple mixed with one or two pieces of a fruitwood, usually apple.

16. Remove the lid, and place your meat on the cooking grates. Keep in mind that the top grate cooks approximately 10 to 20°F (5 to 10°C) hotter than the bottom grate.

17. Replace the lid on the WSM, and continue to monitor the temperature. After you place the meat on the grates, the WSM temperature will drop. Be patient, and the temperature will restabilize. Let the top vent remain wide open throughout the cooking process.

(continued)

18. Continue to monitor the temperature of the smoker. Ideally, for low and slow, you want to maintain a cooking temperature between 225 and 275°F (107 and 135°C).

   ★ Throughout the cooking process, you must continue to monitor the temperature of the smoker.

   ★ If the temperature drops lower than 200°F (93°C), you must open one or more bottom vents. Opening the vents allows more oxygen to reach the lit coals, which raises the cooking temperature.

19. After three or four hours, check the water pan. Add more water as necessary. For best results, add hot water instead of cool water, so that the overall cooking temperature does not drop. Be careful not to spill any water onto the hot charcoal!

20. If you want to add sauce, do so only toward the end of the cooking process.

   ★ Apply sauce approximately 40 minutes before the meat finishes cooking. Apply a second coat of sauce 20 minutes before the meat is finished cooking.

CONTROLLING THE TEMPERATURE

The amount of oxygen that reaches the hot charcoal is the primary factor in determining the cooking temperature of the WSM. As more air reaches the charcoal, the temperature increases. If too much air reaches the charcoal, it can be a bit of challenge to bring the temperature back down. Therefore, learning to control the temperature is important.

ADJUSTING THE VENTS

During the cooking process, you'll have to adjust the bottom vents from time to time in order to control the cooking temperature.

   ★ If the temperature falls below the range specified in the recipe, open the bottom vents, which allow more oxygen to reach the hot charcoal. Once the temperature begins to rise, close the bottom vents slightly.

   ★ Typically, you should try adjusting the three bottom vents equally to obtain an even burn of the hot charcoal.

   ★ If you need to, you can manage the WSM temperature using only one vent. This is particularly helpful on windy days. Close the two vents that are most exposed to the wind, and leave the third vent open. (Alternatively, you can set up a windbreak or try moving the cooker.)

   ★ Don't be too fussy when it comes to small temperature variations. As long as you're close to the target temperatures in the recipes, your dishes should be fabulous!

➳ **Opening or closing the vents provides more or less oxygen to the hot charcoal. This is essentially what controls the temperature. It can take a little while for the WSM to respond to these changes. One skill of an experienced backyard cook is understanding when to expect temperature changes to occur, and acting before it's necessary. This way, only small adjustments to the vents will be necessary.**

MONITORING AIR FLOW

If you've closed all three bottom vents and still can't get the temperature to drop, air may still be infiltrating the charcoal ring. If this happens, one likely spot where air is entering might be the lower seam of the middle cooking section and the base of the WSM. Another likely spot is the area around the side access door. If air is entering in either of these two places, try wrapping a blanket around the WSM to dampen the air flow. You can also wrap the WSM in a blanket when you're cooking on very cold days in order to help insulate it.

Another disruptive measure to keep in mind is opening the lid. We know, believe us, we know, that during the cooking process it can be incredibly tempting to lift the lid and peek at how things are coming along. Each and every time you open the lid, heat escapes. As a result, the temperature must restabilize, which increases the time required to cook the food. This little cooking conundrum gives rise to the expression "If you're looking, you ain't cooking." Depending on how long the lid is off, a significant amount of air can enter the WSM, fueling the fire and causing a temperature spike. If you need to remove the lid, do so only briefly!

EMERGENCY EVACUATION

On very rare occasions, the temperature may be far too hot, and no suggestion will be able to help reduce the heat in time to save your food. In these rare occasions, the last resort might be to use the side access door and remove some hot charcoal from the charcoal ring. If you need to go this route, we recommend using heat-resistant gloves, metal tongs and lots of caution! Make absolutely certain that any hot charcoal you remove from the WSM is disposed of safely, such as in an empty metal trash can.

LIST OF ESSENTIAL EQUIPMENT:

★ Grill brush

★ Long-handle basting brush

★ Tongs

★ Heat-resistant gloves

★ Thermometer

★ Injector

★ Food safety gloves

★ Aluminum foil

★ Lighter

CHAPTER ONE

THE SECRETS TO LOW *and* SLOW COOKING ON THE WSM AND OTHER SMOKERS

Generally speaking, the basic definition of barbecue is using charcoal to cook meat over a low heat source for a long period of time. This definition gave rise to the expression "low and slow." Chances are your interest in this topic, more than any other topic, is what brought you to this book. In order to cook traditional barbecue, you will need to learn how to get a long burn from the charcoal. In the world of barbecue, the most widely used technique to achieve long burn times on the WSM was made famous by an individual on the competition barbecue circuit. His name is Jim Minion, and the Minion Method is what most cooks use when making traditional barbecue on the WSM.

Over the years, Jim Minion made small tweaks and changes to his techniques. Naturally, different people learned slightly different things, yet everybody seems to call the technique they know the Minion Method. While there is a lot of lore surrounding the Minion Method, when you get right down to it, the main idea is really pretty simple to grasp. To simplify: You take a small batch of lit charcoal, and place it on top of a large pile of unlit charcoal. The heat from the lit charcoal slowly spreads to the unlit charcoal, giving rise to long burn time. Because there is only a small amount of charcoal burning at any point during the cook process, the WSM maintains a low temperature, usually in the 225–275°F (107–135°C) range. Although you can use any type of charcoal for this cooking method, we prefer to use natural briquettes.

ADVANTAGES OF THE MINION METHOD

★ Ideal for long cooking sessions that last eight or more hours

★ Great for overnight cooking and large pieces of brisket or pork shoulder

★ Cooking can start in about 45 to 60 minutes

★ Usually no need to add additional charcoal during the cooking process

★ Slow and consistent burn holds temperature steady over many hours

★ Less chance for the WSM temperature to run hot

★ Easy to maintain a constant temperature of 225–275°F (107–135°C)

THINGS TO KEEP IN MIND

★ Not acceptable to those who prefer all briquettes to be fully lit during cooking

★ Not for cooking above 275°F (135°C)

MINION METHOD

Remember, the main idea behind the Minion Method is to add a small amount of lit charcoal to a large amount of unlit charcoal in order to obtain a long, slow burn. Rather than list every variation and tweak associated with the method, what we're sharing is our version of it.

1. Adjust the vents so that the bottom vents are fully open, and the top vent is fully open.

2. Fill the charcoal ring all the way to the top with unlit charcoal.

3. Using the charcoal chimney, light 10 to 15 charcoal briquettes.

4. When the briquettes at the top of the chimney start to turn gray, carefully place the hot coals on top of the unlit coals. When placing the hot charcoal in place, we recommend using metal tongs. Stack all the lit coals as close to the middle of the charcoal ring as possible.

5. Allow about 10 minutes for the coals to catch, and then assemble the WSM.

6. Add hot water to the water pan and fill the pan until the water level is about a half inch (13 millimeters) below the top of the pan. Using hot water allows the cooker to come up to temperature quicker, without using more fuel, and helps to give you a longer cook time.

7. When the WSM is within 50°F (10°C) of the desired cooking temperature, close the bottom vents halfway. Wait for the temperature to stabilize and reach the desired temperature (adjust vents accordingly). After the temperature is stable, add the smoke wood through the side access door. Use a pair of tongs so you don't burn yourself!

8. Place the meat you are cooking onto the cooking grates.

9. Check the water pan every three or four hours, and add water as needed; we recommend using hot water. If you add cool water, the cooking temperature of the WSM will need to restabilize, and you will use more fuel to heat up the cool water that's been added.

➤➤ **If the temperature of the cooker is too high, you can dump the water in the pan and add cold water. The cold water will absorb extra heat, and, in turn, should help bring the temp of the cooker down.**

This pretty much sums up our preferred methodology. The method we outlined typically provides about 10 hours of cooking time. On cold, windy or rainy days, it might be less. If you need to add more charcoal during the cooking process, we recommend adding a half chimney of hot coals. There are many variations of the Minion Method. Feel free to be adventurous and try other versions!

COMPETITION CHICKEN

Chicken can be one of the harder meat categories to master. In competition barbecue, crispy chicken skin is very hard to attain, and it's even harder to maintain, so we do the next best thing: We try to achieve bite-through skin that also has great flavor. It took a lot of practice, and some trial and error, but now I have a technique that will improve your chicken results. I like to use chicken thighs. The dark meat has more flavor and will retain its moisture long after it cools. This recipe got us First Place Chicken at the Jack Daniel's World Championship "Circle of Champions" with almost a perfect score! We also won the New England BBQ Society's Chicken Team of the Year.

YIELD: 18 SERVINGS ★ COOK TIME: ABOUT 2¼ HOURS

2 cups (475 ml) chicken broth

2 tsp (10 g) accent (MSG)

2 family pack chicken thighs (bone in, skin on) 18 pieces, approximately 5 pounds (2.25 kg) per pack

Smokin' Hoggz Dry Rub (page 23)

1 stick of butter/margarine cut into 18 slices

BBQ Sauce (page 23)

½ cup (120 ml) apple juice

1 tsp (5 g) accent

2 disposable aluminum half pans

Aluminum foil

Spice grinder

Small pump sprayer

2–3 chunks sugar maple

First, combine the chicken broth and accent together, making sure the accent dissolves completely. Store in the fridge until ready to use.

Remove skin from the chicken thighs but don't remove it all the way, one side will come off very easy, the other side will still be attached. Lay out thighs and trim each one into uniform, trapezoid shapes, removing some of the excess fat.

Using a paring knife, scrape the high mounds of excess fat from chicken skins. With the meat side facing up and the skin off the side, sprinkle some of the rub on the bare surface of the thigh and reattach skins (the skin should wrap around the thigh, fully covering the front and about half of the back) securing meat and skin together. Refrigerate for 4 hours to overnight.

Using a meat injector, inject about ½ to 1 ounce (15–30 milliliters) of chicken stock mix into left and right side of thigh. Sprinkle back of each thigh with dry rub and let sit at room temperature for 20 minutes.

Fire up WSM for low and slow cooking (approximately 250°F [121°C]), adding chunks of wood about 5 minutes before chicken goes on. You should have 2 dispoable aluminum half pans. Place 9 pieces of butter/margarine in each pan. Rest one chicken thigh on top of each piece of butter/margarine, skin-side up. Sprinkle tops of thighs with dry rub. Place one pan on the bottom rack and one on the top rack of the WSM and smoke for 1 hour, making sure to switch pans around at the 30-minute mark.

After 1 hour, cover each pan with aluminum foil and continue to cook for 1 hour more, again switching racks at the 30-minute mark. (This process will allow you to get bite-through chicken skin. The internal temperature of the chicken will reach 190°F [88°C], but it's not overcooked. Because the chicken was injected, the meat will be tender and juicy.)

(continued)

➺ Injecting chicken thigh

➺ Seasoning back side of chicken thigh

➺ Seasoning skin side

➺ Dunking chicken in sauce

In a medium saucepan, heat the BBQ sauce.

Remove thighs from smoker. Using tongs or gloved hands, submerge each thigh into warm sauce. Shake off excess sauce and place thighs back in smoker, directly on grill grate. Cook until sauce is set (about 15 minutes). Select your best 6 pieces of chicken to present to the judges.

For the finishing rub, take about 2 tablespoons (30 grams) of the dry rub and 1 teaspoon (5 grams) of accent and put them into the spice grinder. Grind until you get a powder-like consistency. Take a pinch of the finishing rub and lightly sprinkle onto each piece of chicken. With a small pump sprayer, spray each piece of chicken with apple juice to help blend in the finishing rub.

SMOKIN' HOGGZ DRY RUB

I think everyone needs a good dry rub in their barbecue bag of tricks to help add a little bit of flavor to the meat. A good dry rub has to be well balanced with the sweet, the heat and a touch of the savory. This rub does just that. Go ahead and give it a try!

YIELD: ABOUT 2 CUPS (480 G)

½ cup (95 g) white sugar
½ cup (100 g) brown sugar
¼ cup (35 g) ancho chili powder
¼ cup (60 g) kosher salt
2 tbsp (15 g) chipotle powder
2 tbsp (15 g) paprika
1 tbsp (10 g) black pepper
2 tsp (10 g) garlic powder
2 tsp (5 g) onion powder
1 tsp (5 g) white pepper
½ tsp allspice

Mix all of the ingredients together and store in an airtight container.

BBQ SAUCE

Barbecue sauce and slow cooked meat is a finely matched pair that goes together like peanut butter and jelly! Most everyone loves barbecue sauce. The key is that you want the sauce to complement the meat—not overpower it. Ideally, you want to apply sauce toward the end of the cooking process. Apply the sauce 30 minutes before the meat comes out of the cooker, and then again with 15 minutes remaining. Remember, you only need to apply a thin layer of sauce on the surface of the meat. The idea is to create layers of flavor. Here is a pretty simple sauce recipe that I think works well with any low and slow cooked meat.

YIELD: ABOUT 2½ CUPS (600 G)

1 cup (240 g) ketchup
½ cup (590 ml) cider vinegar
¼ cup (85 g) molasses
1 tbsp (20 g) Worcestershire sauce
1½ cups (300 g) packed light brown sugar
2 tbsp (12 g) chili powder
1 tbsp (15 g) kosher salt
2 tsp (5 g) coarse black pepper
1 tsp (5 g) garlic powder
1 tsp (5 g) onion powder

In a saucepan on medium heat mix all of the ingredients and simmer for about 15 minutes. Cool and store in the fridge.

➣ For an interesting twist, you can use honey instead of molasses. Honey isn't as rich as molasses, so it provides a more subtle flavor.

COMPETITION RIBS

Ribs are what led me into this obsession with competition barbecue. I started using St. Louis style ribs in competition because they are meatier and have a little bit more fat content than the baby back ribs more commonly found at restaurants. When cooked right, spareribs are juicy, tender and oh so flavorful. Here is my recipe that has helped us win the New England BBQ Society Ribs title of "Team of the Year" three years in a row!

YIELD: 4 RACKS ★ COOK TIME: 4–4½ HOURS

---

4 racks of St. Louis cut spareribs
Smokin' Hoggz Dry Rub (page 23)
16 ounces (455 g) honey
2 cups (400 g) brown sugar
8 tbsp (115 g) butter
2 cups (480 g) BBQ Sauce (page 23)

Heavy duty (HD) aluminum foil

Set up your WSM for low and slow cooking (250–275°F [121–135°C]) and use about 4 good-sized chunks of apple and maple wood. Add the wood just prior to putting the ribs on.

Lay the ribs out with meat side facing down, apply rub to back side of ribs and let set up for about 10 minutes. Flip over and apply rub to meat side, let rub set on ribs for about 15 minutes and then apply another coating of rub. Let them sit for another 30 minutes.

Put two racks on the bottom grate and two on the top grate. After about 90 minutes, switch up the ribs from top to bottom and vice versa. Continue cooking for another 90 minutes.

Lay out four sheets of the HD foil, apply 2 ounces (60 grams) of honey, a ¼ cup (50 grams) brown sugar and 2 tablespoons (30 grams) of butter. Then lay the ribs meat side down, apply 2 ounces (60 grams) of honey, a ¼ cup (50 grams) of brown sugar and a ½ cup (120 grams) of BBQ sauce and wrap tightly; repeat for the other three racks.

Return to the WSM and cook for about 1 more hour; check ribs for doneness.

(To check if ribs are done, look at the back side of the ribs. First the meat will have shrunk from the bone about ¼ to ½ inch [5 to 12 millimeters] and secondly the bones will start to pop through on the back side.)

If ribs are done, remove from WSM and open foil to let them vent for about 10 minutes. This will stop them from cooking any further.

Take about ½ cup (120 milliliters) of juices from foil and ½ cup (120 grams) of BBQ sauce and use this as your glaze.

Cut ribs and serve.

COMPETITION PORK

The meat used in the competition pork category comes from the pork shoulder. The pork shoulder is comprised of two pieces: the pork shoulder and the pork butt. Pork shoulder and pork butt have a very high intramuscular fat content. This fat provides both the challenge of cooking and the reward of eating barbecue pork. The challenge is rendering the fat down without overcooking the meat. The reward is a tender, moist and flavorful product that is hard to beat. This was the pork recipe that got us the call, in which we eventually went on to win the 2011 Jack Daniel's World Barbecue Championships.

YIELD: ABOUT 30 SERVINGS ★ COOK TIME: APPROXIMATELY 10–12 HOURS

---

2 (8–10 pound [4–5 kg]) Boston butts, bone-in

Pork Injection (page 29)

½ cup (120 ml) yellow mustard (or honey mustard)

Smokin' Hoggz Dry Rub (page 23)

Pork Braise (page 29)

1½ cups (360 ml) Head Country Bar-B-Q Sauce

1½ cups (360 ml) Blues Hog Barbecue Sauce

Heavy duty (HD) aluminum foil

4 chunks of apple and sugar maple wood (2 each)

Fire up the WSM and get it ready for low and slow cooking. (approximately 250°F [121°C]). Fill up the water pan to about half using hot water. Do this about 1 hour before you want to put the butts on. This will allow the cooker to get up to temperature. Add the smoke wood at the same time you put the butts on the WSM.

Trim the butts of any extra or loose fat but keep the fat cap on. This will help protect the butt and keep all moisture in. Remember fat is flavor.

Take half of the injection liquid and start to inject the meat. Make sure the majority of the injection goes into the muscle opposite the bone (a.k.a. money muscle) and the muscles around the bone. The reason for the term "money muscle" is that if it is cooked perfectly, you'll be in the money every time at a contest.

Now rub down the entire butt with the mustard; you don't need too much, all this is doing is making a nice surface for the rub to adhere to. After you coated the butt with mustard, generously apply the dry rub.

Wrap the butts in plastic wrap and put into the fridge or cooler until about an hour before they go on the WSM.

An hour before the butts go onto the cooker, remove them from the refrigerator or cooler and apply another generous coating of rub. Let the re-rubbed meat sit at room temperature until ready to go on the WSM.

At the same time the butts go on, add the wood chunks. Place butts on the WSM, fat side up. Place one on the top grate and the other on the bottom grate. Cook the butts until they reach an internal temperature of about 160–170°F (71–77°C) (approximately 6 hours).

(continued)

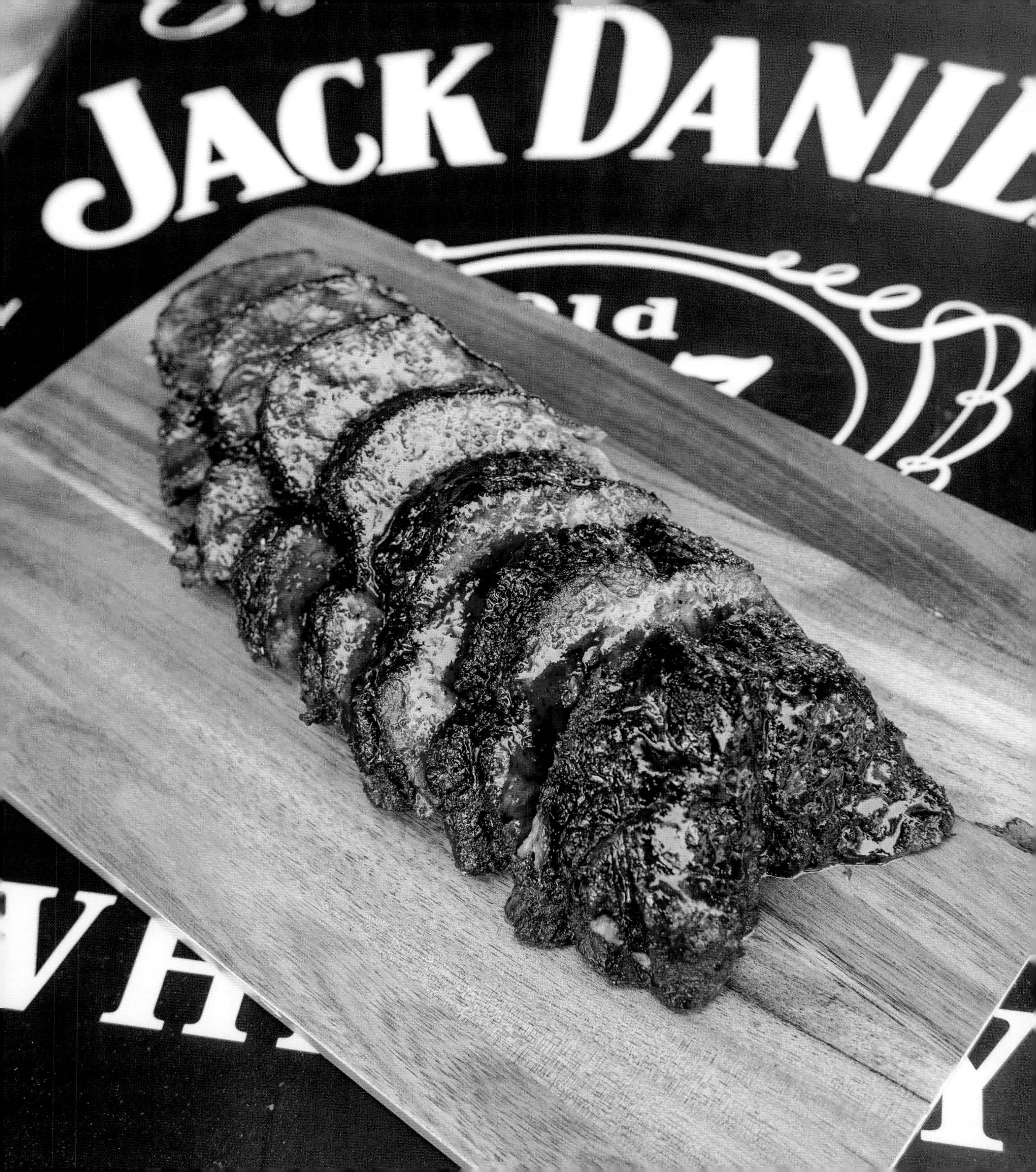
JACK DANI

➤ Applying sauce to money muscle

➤ Slicing money muscle

Once the butts have reached the desired internal temperature, they are ready to wrap in foil. Lay out two sheets of HD foil (big enough to fully wrap each butt). Place each butt fat side down, add the pork braise onto each butt and then wrap butts completely with foil and return to WSM and cook until an internal temperature of about 190–195°F (88–91°C) or until probe tender.

Remove the butts from WSM, open foil and allow the steam to dissipate (about 10 minutes). This will help stop the cooking process. During this time, mix the two BBQ sauces together and apply a coating to the top surface of the butt. Close foil and let rest for a minimum of one hour; you can use a dry empty cooler lined with some old towels.

When the pork is ready to serve, cut off the front muscle (money muscle), slice into ¾-inch (2-centimeter) slices and brush each slice with sauce. Remove the bone and all the meat around the bone, place chunks into a half pan and pour super-hot BBQ sauce all over it. Cover with foil and let sit for 15 minutes.

➤ **Wrapping meat in foil does a couple things. It allows you to add more flavors to the meat by catching juices and adding marinade, and it helps quicken the cooking process.**

PORK INJECTION

An injection is a great way to add more flavor and to help keep the meat moist and tender. This pork injection will absolutely bring your pork to the next level.

YIELD: ABOUT 3 CUPS (710 ML)

1 cup (240 ml) apple juice or white grape juice
2 tbsp (30 g) kosher salt
½ cup (120 ml) water
½ cup (100 g) brown sugar
1 tsp (2 g) cayenne pepper
2 tbsp (30 ml) soy sauce
¼ cup (60 ml) apple cider vinegar
¼ cup (60 g) Amesphos phosphates

Combine all of the ingredients and stir until salt and sugar are completely dissolved.

PORK BRAISE

A braise is another fantastic method of adding more flavor to any meat you cook, and it's also a great way to help further tenderize tough cuts of meat.

YIELD: ABOUT 1½ CUPS (350 ML)

1 bottle of Stubb's Pork Marinade, strained
¼ cup (60 ml) apple juice
1 tbsp (15 g) Smokin' Hoggz Dry Rub (page 23)

Mix all of the ingredients and heat just before using.

COMPETITION BRISKET

In my opinion, brisket is not only the hardest meat category to cook, it's also the hardest meat category to obtain consistent results. When brisket is cooked perfectly, it's the juiciest, most tender, most flavorful piece of meat you will ever eat. There are two pieces of meat associated with brisket: the flat and the point. The flat is just that, a flat, rectangular piece of meat that makes up the majority of the brisket. It is the leaner of the two pieces, and is what you will be cutting into slices. The point is the other part of the brisket. It lies across part of the flat and is a fattier piece of meat. You can also slice this section, but it's better for making chopped chunks of meat or for serving burnt ends. This brisket recipe has gotten us Fifth Place (out of more than 500 teams) at the American Royal Open Contest, and First Place Brisket Team of the Year for New England BBQ Society two years in a row.

YIELD: ABOUT 30 SERVINGS ★ COOK TIME: APPROXIMATELY 10–12 HOURS

15–17 pounds (6.5–8 kg) brisket
Brisket Injection (page 34)
Smokin' Hoggz Dry Rub (page 23)
Brisket Marinade (page 34)
BBQ Sauce (page 23)

HD aluminum foil
Half pan, disposable
4 chunks of hickory or oak

Trim all the loose fat and silver skin from the flat side of the brisket. Remove most of the fat from the point. The reason you are removing all the fat from the outside side of the point is because the point is loaded with fat all throughout, and it would be difficult to render all that internal fat. Plus, you want a nice surface to apply the rub and get that flavorful bark for those burnt ends!

Next, inject the brisket with the brisket injection. Starting at the opposite end from the point, and perpendicular to the grain of the meat, inject every 2 inches (5 centimeters) going in a checkerboard pattern, and then do the same thing for the point.

Now, go ahead and season the brisket with the rub; brisket can handle a lot of rub so be generous. Wrap in plastic wrap and place in fridge or cooler until about an hour before putting it on the WSM.

About an hour before the brisket goes onto the cooker, remove from fridge or cooler and reapply rub and let the brisket sit on the counter or table until ready for the cooker.

Fire up the WSM for low and slow cooking (approximately 250°F [121°C]), and fill the water pan with hot water to about ½ inch (13 millimeters) from the top of the pan. Add smoke wood the same time you put the brisket on to cook.

At the same time you're putting the brisket on the WSM, throw in the wood chunks. Then place the brisket on the top rack of the WSM fat side up, and cook until an internal temp of 160–170°F (71–76°C).

(continued)

➳ Making burnt endz

➳ Slicing the flat

➳ Saucing the burnt endz

➳ Saucing the slices

COMPETITION BRISKET (CONTINUED)

When brisket reaches the desired internal temp, it's ready for wrapping. Remove it from the cooker and lay out a large piece of HD foil (big enough to wrap the entire brisket). Place the brisket on the foil, fat side down, and add the brisket marinade. Wrap brisket completely and put it back on the WSM until you reach an internal temp of approximately 195–200°F (91–93°C) or until probe tender.

Remove brisket from the WSM and vent foil to release steam (approximately 10 minutes) and to stop the cooking process. At this time, take some of the BBQ sauce and coat the surface of the brisket. Wrap brisket back up and rest it in a dry empty cooler for a minimum of one hour.

Time to make some burnt endz! Take your brisket out of the cooler and separate the flat from the point. This is done by taking a large slicing knife and slicing along the fat that is in between the two pieces. If the brisket is cooked right there should be no resistance in separating the two pieces (like a hot knife going through room temperature butter).

Wrap the flat back up; take the point and cut it into 1-inch (2.5-centimeter) cubes. Place the cubes into a half pan, add some BBQ sauce and put back onto the WSM for an additional 20 minutes.

While you're waiting for the burnt ends to finish, go ahead and start slicing the flat. Return the sliced brisket back to its juices in the foil cover, and let sit until burnt ends are done.

➺ **When you cook the brisket fat side up, the fat renders down into the meat during the cooking process. This creates a more flavorful, tender and juicy piece of meat. If you cook with the fat side down, the finished product will contain more bark on the edge of the meat. Try cooking brisket both ways to see which way you like better!**

➺ **For brisket, you want to check the internal temperature in three different places: the point, in the middle of the flat and at the end of the flat. You're looking for a temperature of about 195°F (91°C) in the flat and 200–205°F (93–96°C) in the point.**

BRISKET INJECTION

This injection will help add a ton of flavor and help keep your brisket super moist. Plus, it will really enhance that beefy flavor of the brisket.

YIELD: 2½ CUPS (590 ML)

---

1 cup (240 ml) beef broth
1 cup (240 ml) water
1 tbsp (15 ml) beef broth concentrate
2 tbsp (20 g) Worcestershire sauce
¼ cup (60 g) phosphates
2 cloves garlic, roughly chopped
1 onion, chopped

The day before in a sauce pan over medium heat mix all ingredients, cool and store in fridge. When ready to use, strain out the garlic and onion.

BRISKET MARINADE

This marinade will act like a braise and really add a ton of flavor to your brisket. We like to use this marinade on our brisket to stay one step ahead of the competition!

YIELD: 2½ CUPS (590 ML)

---

12 ounce (355 ml) can of dark beer
¼ cup (60 ml) apple cider vinegar
¼ cup (70 g) Worcestershire sauce
1 tbsp (15 ml) beef broth concentrate (sodium free)
1 tbsp (10 g) garlic powder
1 tbsp (10 g) onion powder
1 tbsp (15 g) brisket rub
1 tsp (3 g) celery seed
2 tsp (10 g) MSG
1 tsp (2 g) cayenne pepper

Mix and heat right before use.

SMOKIN' HOGGZ ALL-PURPOSE RUB

This was one of the first rubs I developed a few years back. I primarily used it on chicken, pork and seafood and only during grilling events. This is a very well-rounded rub with some great flavor, and it will definitely bring a little pop to anything you cook.

YIELD: ABOUT 3 CUPS (725 G)

¼ cup (30 g) ground chipotle powder
¼ cup (50 g) Turbinado sugar
¼ cup (30 g) ground ancho chili powder
¼ cup (30 g) paprika
¼ cup (60 g) kosher salt
1 tbsp (5 g) ground cumin
1 tbsp (10 g) onion powder
1 tbsp (5 g) dried thyme
1 tsp (1 g) dried marjoram
1 tsp (2 g) cayenne
2 tbsp (15 g) green peppercorns, crushed
1 tbsp (10 g) ground white pepper
1 tsp (2 g) celery seed (or ½ tsp celery seed powder)
½ tsp ground allspice
½ tsp cinnamon
½ tsp ginger

Mix all of the ingredients and store them in an airtight container.

➼ You can apply rubs anywhere from an hour before cooking the meat to mere moments before the meat hits the grill. As a general rule, you should try to apply a rub one hour before you cook.

ABTS (ATOMIC BUFFALO TURDS) STUFFED WITH BRISKET BURNT ENDZ

Starting out in the BBQ world I kept hearing about these things called ABTs. Then I had the pleasure of trying one, and oh, my god I was hooked! In my opinion, these small tasty morsels are the crack of the barbecue world. Here is my interpretation of the ABT and what to do with some leftover brisket.

YIELD: 4 SERVINGS ★ COOK TIME: APPROXIMATELY 2 HOURS

8 jalapeños
8 ounces (225 g) cream cheese
Sweet chili sauce
16 pieces of brisket burnt endz (page 30), 1" x 1" (2.5 cm x 2.5 cm) cubes
16 slices of bacon
Smokin' Hoggz All-Purpose Rub (page 35)
½ cup (120 ml) Blues Hog Barbecue Sauce

3–4 chunks of apple wood or sugar maple

Heat your WSM for low and slow cooking (approximately 250°F [121°C]). This is only going to be a short cook so you can use the Mini-Minion low and slow method, so you don't waste any charcoal. Also, fill your water pan about halfway with hot water.

Cut jalapeños in half and remove the seeds and vein; if you like spicy, you can leave the vein alone. Take about ½ ounce (15 grams) of the cream cheese and spread it in the cavity of the sliced jalapeño. Then use about one spoonful of sweet chili sauce and spread on top of the cream cheese layer. Now, you'll want to take the burnt end cube and cut it in half and place each half next to each other on top of the sweet chili sauce/cream cheese. Take one of the slices of bacon; starting from the stem end of the pepper, wrap the bacon around in a spiral pattern, making sure the end of the bacon is on the bottom of the pepper. An easy way to do this is to lay the slice of bacon out in a straight line and place the pepper on an angle and roll pepper up in the bacon.

Apply the Smokin' Hoggz All Purpose Rub all over the wrapped pepper. Place the peppers on the top rack of the WSM and cook for approximately 2 hours or until the bacon is done.

While the peppers are cooking, take the BBQ sauce and pour it into a squeeze bottle and place bottle into a pot of hot water (this you can do about 30 minutes before the peppers are done).

About 15 minutes before the peppers are done, apply the BBQ sauce in a zigzag motion, put cover back on and let the sauce set for about 15 minutes. Remove the peppers from the WSM and let them rest for about 5–10 minutes, then serve.

➡➡ **Essentially, the Mini-Minion Method uses less charcoal than the method outlined earlier in this book for a shorter burn time. Use one unlit charcoal chimney in the charcoal ring, then light 10 charcoal briquettes. When the 10 briquettes are ready, dump them on top of the unlit charcoal.**

ARMADILLO EGGS

I didn't know armadillos laid eggs! HAHAHA, they don't really, but these are spicy meat treats I love to make when I'm hosting a party or tailgating at a football game. People just love these tasty little nuggets. So, armadillo eggs aren't actually eggs, they're just called eggs because the cheese filling in the center looks like the yolk of an egg, and when fully assembled they are shaped like an egg.

YIELD: 24 ARMADILLO EGGS ★ COOK TIME: APPROXIMATELY 1 HOUR

---

8 ounces (230 g) cream cheese, softened
1 cup (113 g) cheddar cheese
2 garlic cloves, finely diced
6 jalapeños (cut in half, then each side cut in half)
1 pound (455 g) Jimmy Dean sausage
1 pound (455 g) ground Italian sausage
½ pound (230 g) ground chorizo
Smokin' Hoggz All-Purpose Rub (page 35)
24 slices bacon
1 cup (240 g) ranch dressing

Get your WSM heated up for low and slow cooking (approximately 250°F [121°C]), filling the water pan about halfway with warm to hot water.

Mix together the cream cheese, cheddar cheese and garlic until well blended. Taste and add salt if needed.

Remove the stems from the jalapeños and cut in half lengthwise. Scoop out the seeds and then cut the sliced jalapeños in half, so one jalapeño should get you 4 quarters. Place about a teaspoon (5 grams) of the cream cheese filling in each jalapeño quarter. Take about ⅓ cup (45 grams) of the sausage and pat it into a 3-inch (7-centimeter) circle and place the stuffed jalapeño in the center of the sausage. Wrap the sausage around the stuffed jalapeño until it's completely covered, and form into an egg shape. Wrap each egg with one strip of bacon making sure the seam is down. Season each egg with dry rub.

Place sausage-wrapped jalapeños directly on the top grate of the WSM. Cook for 1–1½ hours, or until the sausage is cooked.

Serve with ranch dressing.

BACON WRAPPED STUFFED BURNT ENDZ

The best thing about a BBQ is the leftovers. What could possibly be better than taking the "golden nugget" of a brisket burnt end, stuffing it and wrapping it in bacon? Nothing—that's what's better than bacon wrapped stuffed burnt endz—nothing.

YIELD: 6 SERVINGS ★ COOK TIME: APPROXIMATELY 1 HOUR

12 (1" x 1" [2.5 cm x 2.5 cm]) burnt end chunks from brisket (page 30)
6 ounces (170 g) cream cheese
4 ounces (115 g) pickled jalapeños slices
24 slices of bacon
Smokin' Hoggz All-Purpose Rub (page 35)
½ cup (120 g) BBQ Sauce (page 23)

Preheat your WSM to 250°F (121°C) (low and slow cooking), and fill your water pan about halfway with hot water.

Slice burnt end in half so you have 2 pieces. Spread about ½ ounce (15 grams) of cream cheese on one half of burnt end and top with 1 or 2 jalapeño slices. Put burnt end back together and wrap each one with two pieces of bacon. Make sure entire burnt end is wrapped with bacon.

Season with the rub and place pieces on the top grate. Cook for approximately 1 hour or until bacon is browned.

While still on smoker and with about 15 minutes left to cook, glaze with BBQ sauce and continue to cook. Remove from WSM and let rest for 10 minutes.

BACON WRAPPED LITTLE SMOKIES

This is a great appetizer to serve at your next party. Slightly sweet and very savory, this unbelievable little snack will bring ear-to-ear smiles to the faces of your friends and family.

YIELD: ABOUT 10 SERVINGS (4 PER SERVING) ★ COOK TIME: APPROXIMATELY 1 HOUR

1 pound (455 g) bacon
1 pound (455 g) little smokies sausages
Smokin' Hoggz All-Purpose Rub (page 35)
1 cup (200 g) brown sugar
1 stick of butter, sliced

1 disposable half pan

Preheat your WSM to 275°F (135°C).

Cut each bacon slice into 3 to 4 pieces. Wrap each sausage with a piece of bacon; secure with a toothpick. Place these in a half pan. Sprinkle evenly with rub and brown sugar. Add butter and cook for 45–60 minutes or until bacon is browned and brown sugar melts and forms a sauce.

STUFFED MUSHROOMS WITH ITALIAN SAUSAGE

Stuffed mushrooms are always a big hit at get-togethers and holiday parties. The earthiness of the mushroom and savory flavors from sausage make this one of my favorite side dishes.

YIELD: 12 SERVINGS ★ COOK TIME: APPROXIMATELY 2 HOURS

---

1 pound (455 g) ground Italian sausage

24 mushrooms (baby portobello)

½ medium onion, chopped

4 cloves garlic, chopped

2 pounds (910 g) frozen chopped spinach, well drained

⅓ pound (150 g) goat cheese

3 tbsp (45 ml) olive oil

2 tbsp (8 g) bread crumbs

3 tbsp (35 g) Parmesan cheese

¾ cup (180 ml) dark beer (the good stuff)

1 shot (about 1½ oz [40 ml]) Jack Daniel's

Salt and pepper (to taste)

1 cup (200 g) apple wood chips

(Note, you can prepare the stuffing ahead of time and store in the fridge.) To make the stuffing, brown the Italian sausage in a large skillet. Wash the mushrooms and carefully remove the stems. Set the mushrooms aside and finely chop the stems. Add the stems, onion and garlic to the sausage and sauté over medium heat until the onions are translucent. Remove excess fat (if any) from the mixture. Reduce the heat to medium-low and add the drained spinach. Stir several minutes until the spinach is completely incorporated. Add the goat cheese and stir until it melts into the mixture. Taste and adjust seasonings with salt and pepper. Reserve the mixture (allowing it to cool slightly).

Brush the mushroom caps with olive oil (top and bottom) and sprinkle them with salt. Place them in a grill safe pan (I used an aluminum foil pan) stem side up. Add enough stuffing to make a heaping pile in each mushroom cap. Sprinkle bread crumbs and Parmesan cheese over the stuffing. Carefully add the beer to the bottom of the pan.

Prepare the WSM for low and slow cooking. Add the apple wood chips to a small bowl and pour one shot of the whiskey over them. Add water to cover and set aside (at least a half hour). Add the pan of mushrooms to the WSM. Drain the wood chips and add to the hot coals. Cover and cook for 60 minutes until the mushrooms are tender and the toppings are slightly crunchy. Rotate once during the cooking time. The actual cooking time will depend upon the size of your mushrooms and the initial temperature of your stuffing.

➥ **You could spice this up with some peppers or hot sauce in the stuffing mixture.**

BRISKET CHILI

What do you do with all the leftover brisket from competition? Make some chili of course! I love making chili almost as much as I love eating chili. This recipe has won chili contests and multiple People's Choice awards over the last few years. It's sure to satisfy and keep you and your friends warm on cold winter days.

YIELD: 16 SERVINGS ★ COOK TIME: APPROXIMATELY 1½ TO 2 HOURS

1 pound (455 g) ground sirloin
½ pound (230 g) ground chorizo
½ pound (230 g) ground linguica
1 pound (455 g) leftover brisket (page 30), cubed
½ onion, diced
4 cloves garlic
Salt and pepper
4 chipotle peppers in adobo sauce, diced
28 ounce (795 g) can diced tomatoes
8 ounce (230 g) can tomato puree
1 (12 ounce [340 ml]) dark beer
¼ cup (30 g) paprika
2 tbsp (15 g) cumin
2 tsp (5 g) chipotle powder
¼ cup (30 g) ancho powder
1 tbsp (90 g) oregano
1 bar Mexican chocolate
¼ cup (30 g) masa (corn flour)
8 ounces (230 g) shredded cheddar cheese
8 ounces (230 g) sour cream

1 large Dutch oven
2 chunks of sugar maple wood

Set up your WSM for low and slow cooking (approximately 250–275°F [121–135°C]), and fill your water pan three-quarters full with hot water. Add the smoke wood about 5 minutes before adding chili.

Place an empty Dutch oven on the top grate of WSM, and coat the inside with some olive oil. This will pre-heat the Dutch oven so you won't lose any cooking time by putting it in cold.

Brown ground sirloin over medium heat in a pan and add chorizo and linguica.

In the Dutch oven combine all ingredients except the cheese and mix well. Put it on a 275°F (135°C) WSM and cook uncovered for about an hour; cover then cook for about another 1½–2 hours.

Serve with some shredded cheddar cheese and sour cream.

SMOKED JALAPEÑOS (CHIPOTLES)

Chipotle chilies are smoked and dried jalapeño peppers. The unique combination of smoky flavor with peppery heat makes chipotles perfect for numerous uses. They can be put in soups and sauces, served with beans or ground into a fine powder that you add to spice rubs or sprinkle over vegetables.

There are several ways to prepare chipotles, but first you must begin with nicely ripened jalapeño peppers. Try to look for jalapeños that are firm without any soft spots. They should have a good, bright color without any loose stems (an indication that they were picked too long ago). The fresher the peppers, the better the results.

YIELD: 16–24 SERVINGS ★ COOK TIME: APPROXIMATELY 6–8 HOURS

16–24 fresh red or green jalapeños

5–6 chunks of smoking wood (hickory)

Get the WSM heated up to maintain a temperature of about 180°F (82°C) and use an empty foiled water pan.

Rinse peppers under cold water and pat dry. Now would be a good time to put on some food grade gloves, and don't touch your eyes, nose or face; you may not like the results!

Cut off the top of each pepper to remove the stem, and then cut in half lengthwise. This will help with faster drying in the cooker.

Spray the cooking grates with non-stick spray and arrange the peppers cut-side up.

Place the peppers on the top grate and add one piece of smoke wood, checking in every hour and add another piece of smoke wood—you'll probably be looking at about a 6–8 hour cook.

Remove peppers from the WSM and let air dry for about 1 to 2 days to really make sure they have dried out. Store in an airtight container for later use.

KICKED-UP BBQ BAKED BEANS

You can't have BBQ without having some sort of beans! And being from Boston, I certainly better know how to make baked beans. These beans are my take on the traditional New England baked beans and are sure to please your friends and family!

YIELD: 8 SERVINGS ★ COOK TIME: APPROXIMATELY 3 HOURS

2 large (28-ounce [800 g]) cans baked beans, drained

1 cup (240 g) Sweet Baby Ray's Original Barbeque Sauce

¼ sweet onion, diced

½ cup (115 g) salt pork

½ pound (230 g) thick-cut bacon, cooked and diced

2 tbsp (30 g) Smokin' Hoggz Dry Rub (page 23)

1 jalapeño pepper, seeded and chopped finely (If you don't like your beans spicy, you can leave out the jalapeños)

1 disposable aluminum half pan

2 chunks of apple wood

Set up your WSM for low and slow cooking (approximately 250°F [121°C]).

Combine all of the ingredients into a disposable half pan and place on the top rack of the WSM. Add the apple wood chunks and cook for about 2 hours uncovered; stir after about an hour to add some of that great smoke flavor from the apple wood and continue cooking. Stir them up again and cover; cook for an additional hour.

Remove and let rest for about 30 minutes. Serve as a great side dish with your favorite BBQ meats.

MAC & CHEESE

Growing up, my mother always made mac & cheese, and not that stuff from the box. This was the real deal. It was very simple, but so delicious! It was basically elbow macaroni, two different cheddar cheeses (white and yellow), milk, flour and a cracker crumb top, and my mom cooked it in a big red bowl. I would always go for the sides of the bowl, because that's where I could find all the well-done, melted cheese! It was always the best for leftovers the next day. So here's my take on one of America's most loved comfort foods.

YIELD: 8 SERVINGS ★ COOK TIME: APPROXIMATELY 1 HOUR

1 (16 ounce [455 g]) package elbow macaroni

1 stick butter

¼ cup (25 g) all-purpose flour

3 cups (710 ml) milk

½ cup (40 g) Parmesan cheese, shredded

1 tsp (5 g) salt

½ tsp black pepper

2 cups (230 g) extra sharp cheddar cheese, shredded

1½ cups (165 g) Gouda cheese, shredded

1½ cups (165 g) Gruyère cheese, shredded

1½ cups (216 g) Fontina cheese, shredded

1 pound (455 g) bacon, cooked and chopped

1 sleeve crackers, crushed into crumbs

1 (8 ounce [230 g]) package cream cheese, cut into chunks

1 disposable aluminum half pan
1 chunk of apple wood

Fire up your WSM for low and slow cooking (approximately 275°F [121°C]), and fill your water pan half way with hot water. Add the smoke wood at the same time you put the mac & cheese on the WSM.

Cook pasta according to package directions.

In a medium saucepan, melt ½ stick of butter, and whisk flour into the butter. Cook over medium heat for 2 minutes, until sauce is bubbly and thick. Whisk in milk and bring to a boil. Cook 5 minutes until thickened. Stir in Parmesan and cream cheese until mixture is smooth. Add salt and pepper.

In a large bowl, combine 1 cup (115 grams) cheddar, 1 cup (108 grams) Gouda, 1 cup (108 grams) Gruyère, 1 cup (135 grams) Fontina, pasta, bacon and cream sauce. Pour mixture into an aluminum half pan coated with nonstick cooking spray. Sprinkle the top with remaining cheese.

For crumb topping, melt remaining butter and add cracker crumbs, mix well. Sprinkle onto mac & cheese.

Place on the top grate of the WSM and cook for about an hour at 275°F (121°C), until brown, bubbly and delicious.

THREE POTATO BACON AND CHEESE CASSEROLE

Let's see … potatoes, bacon and cheese … all cooked together … to create one of the ultimate comfort foods! We came up with this recipe a few years ago at a contest for a savory bacon dish entry. This dish got us a top 5 call and a top 3 overall for the contest.

YIELD: 8 SERVINGS ★ COOK TIME: APPROXIMATELY 2 HOURS

1 large sweet potato
1 large Japanese sweet potato
1 large russet potato
Olive oil
2 pounds (910 g) bacon, diced and cooked
8 ounces (230 g) Gruyère cheese, shredded
8 ounces (230 g) Fontina cheese, shredded
8 ounces (230 g) cheddar cheese, shredded
Salt and pepper

Dutch oven

Set up your WSM for low and slow cooking (approximately 275°F [121°C]).

Slice all three potatoes thin using a mandolin—you're looking for a thickness of about ⅛ inch (3 millimeters).

Coat the bottom of a Dutch oven with some olive oil.

Layer the three different kinds of potatoes, top with bacon and cheeses and season each layer with salt and pepper. Repeat layering until all of the ingredients are used.

Cook on the top rack of the WSM for about one hour, cover and cook for another 1–2 hours or until potatoes are soft (you can stick a knife thru with no resistance).

Remove and let rest for about 30 minutes. Slice into wedges and serve.

SMOKED CORN

Most of us weekend warrior BBQr's are crazy about the meats (ribs, brisket, pork butt and chicken) but we never really think about cooking sides in the smoker, much less something like corn on the cob. Let me tell you though, if you want to step it up a few notches, then you have to start thinking about the veggies. Corn is best when it's fresh; so don't buy it too far ahead of time. I like to buy corn the same day I am going to cook it.

YIELD: 6 SERVINGS ★ COOK TIME: APPROXIMATELY 2 HOURS

6 ears of corn
12 tbsp (175 g) unsalted butter
Salt and pepper to taste

2 chunks of apple wood

Fire up the WSM for low and slow cooking (approximately 225–250°F [107–121°C]), and add the smoke wood about 15 minutes before cooking.

Peel off most of the husk from the corn leaving only 1 or 2 layers on. Then carefully peel them back but leave them attached; clean all the silk off and rinse them well. Spread butter all over them with a little salt and pepper. Put the thin layer of husk back on and take a thin piece of the discarded husk and use it like a piece of string to tie the end closed. Put these on the WSM for about 2 hours.

SPICY, SWEET SMOKED ALMONDS

Smoked nuts are a tasty snack to prepare on the Weber Smokey Mountain Cooker. A lot of the roasted nut recipes that are prepared in the oven can be done on a smoker with your favorite wood to help kick things up a bit. Smoked almonds are great to serve at parties or just to have as a simple snack. They also make great holiday gifts.

YIELD: ABOUT 2 CUPS (340 G) ★ COOK TIME: APPROXIMATELY 30 MINUTES

¼ cup (85 g) honey
1 tbsp (15 g) organic white sugar
1 tbsp (15 g) butter, melted
½ tsp salt
½ tsp ancho chili powder
¼ tsp chipotle powder
¼ tsp allspice
½ tsp cinnamon
2 cups (340 g) whole almonds

1 chunk sugar maple wood
1 disposable aluminum pan
Cooking spray

Fire up you cooker for the upper end of low and slow cooking (approximately 275–300°F [135–149°C]). This time leave the water pan empty. Add the smoke wood about 5 minutes before cooking.

In a bowl mix up all of the ingredients except the almonds; the result should be a nice sticky paste. Add the almonds and mix until well coated. Spray an aluminum pan with cooking spray. Pour the almonds onto the pan and make sure they are in a single layer.

Place the pan on the top rack of the WSM, and cook for about 30 minutes. Shake the pan a couple of times during the cook to mix the nuts up a little.

Remove from cooker and let cool for about 20 minutes. As the nuts cool they will most likely stick together, so you'll want to break them up a bit. Serve or store in an airtight container.

BUTTERY SMOKED CABBAGE

This smoked cabbage is the perfect complement or side dish to add to any barbecue meat you are cooking. You can cook the cabbage right along with the meat and if you time things right, everything will be ready at the same time. Smoked cabbage is sort of like a cross between coleslaw and sauerkraut, with a fantastic smoky flavor—you know you want to try it!

YIELD: 4 SERVINGS ★ COOK TIME: APPROXIMATELY 4–5 HOURS

---

1 large head of cabbage

Salt and pepper

¼ cup (40 g) sweet onion, diced (I use Vidalia when in season)

1 stick of butter, sliced and at room temp

½ cup (115 g) uncooked pancetta, diced

HD aluminum foil

2 chunks apple wood

Set up your WSM for low and slow cooking (approximately 250°F [121°C]), and fill your water pan about three-quarters full with hot water. Add your smoke wood at the same time you put the cabbage on the cooker.

Take the head of cabbage and remove the core; you will end up with what looks like a bowl. Make sure it's big enough to hold all of the ingredients. Season the cored out cabbage with salt and pepper. Add the onions and then add the butter. Lastly, top with the pancetta.

Make a ring with the aluminum foil, and place cabbage in the center. This will allow the head of cabbage to remain upright during the entire cook. Cook for about 4–5 hours or until the cabbage is tender. When done, take off the cooker, and remove any blackened leaves. Cut into quarters and serve.

BACON-STUFFED SAUSAGE FATTY WRAPPED IN BACON

What could be better than a cheesy bacon mixture, wrapped inside of sausage, then wrapped again in bacon and cooked to perfection? Your guess is as good as mine. Here is the ultimate in bacony delicious madness.

YIELD: 12–16 SERVINGS ★ COOK TIME: APPROXIMATELY 2½ HOURS

1 pound (455 g) breakfast sausage (Jimmy Dean)
1 pound (455 g) sweet Italian sausage
½ pound (230 g) ground chorizo
2 pounds (910 g) bacon, diced and cooked
½–1 cup (70–140 g) Velveeta cheese
1 pound (455 g) bacon, uncooked
Smokin' Hoggz Dry Rub (page 23)
1 cup (240 g) BBQ Sauce (page 23)

HD aluminum foil
Cooking spray

For this recipe you will be cooking on the upper end of the low and slow spectrum, somewhere around 275°F (135°C). Fill the water pan about three-quarters full with warm water. Add your smoke wood about 5 minutes before putting the fatty on.

Mix all the sausage together. Put the mixture into a gallon-sized bag, and flatten out until the mixture reaches all sides of the bag and is equal thickness throughout (about ½ inch [13 millimeters] thick). Take out of the bag and put it on a sheet of aluminum foil sprayed with non stick cooking spray.

Take the cooked bacon and spread it out over the sausage and add the cheese. Roll the entire thing into a log, and completely season the outside with the dry rub.

Take the uncooked bacon and make a bacon weave; place the sausage log onto the bacon weave and roll weave all the way around the log and season with more dry rub.

Place sausage fatty onto the grate of a preheated grill/smoker at 275°F (135°C), and cook for about 2–2½ hours. You can add any kind of smoke wood you like—I like apple or sugar maple. During the last half hour, brush on your favorite BBQ sauce.

Take the fatty off the cooker and let rest for about one hour. Slice into 1–1½-inch (2.5–4-centimeter) slices, serve and enjoy.

(continued)

➻ Assembling bacon weave

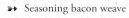

➻ Seasoning bacon weave

➻ Wrapping sausage with bacon weave

➻ Applying sauce

BLUEBERRY BBQ SAUCE

Next time you fire up your grill or smoker and you are looking for a little twist to the traditional BBQ flavors, try using this Blueberry BBQ sauce. It's awesome with chicken and pork, but especially great with any sausage fatty!

YIELD: ABOUT 3 CUPS (720 G) ★ COOK TIME: 20 MINUTES

2 cups (300 g) fresh blueberries
½ cup (120 ml) balsamic vinegar
3 tbsp (40 g) brown sugar
3 tbsp (45 g) ketchup
1 clove garlic, minced
½ tsp kosher salt

Place all of the ingredients into a saucepan, bring to a boil, then lower temp and simmer for 15–20 minutes until it thickens. Remove and let cool. Then puree in a blender or food processor.

STUFFED SAUSAGE FATTY WITH BLUEBERRY

Say what? That's right—a sausage fatty stuffed with blueberry muffin and maple syrup. Sound strange? Well, it was a big hit with the judges and placed second at a few contests. Just wait till you try it, you'll be making this recipe every chance you get!

YIELD: 12–16 SERVINGS ★ COOK TIME: APPROXIMATELY 2½ HOURS

2 pounds (910 g) of breakfast sausage (Jimmy Dean)
1 pound (455 g) sweet Italian sausage
4–6 medium-sized blueberry muffins
1 cup (240 ml) maple syrup
1 pound (455 g) maple bacon
Smokin' Hoggz All-Purpose Rub (page 35)
Blueberry BBQ Sauce (page 61)

HD aluminum foil
Cooking spray

Plastic wrap

For this recipe you will be cooking on the upper end of the low and slow spectrum, somewhere around 275°F (135°C). Fill the water pan about three-quarters full with warm water. Add your smoke wood about 5 minutes before putting the fatty on.

Next, crumble the blueberry muffins in a bowl and add the maple syrup and mix. Place this onto plastic wrap and form into a log about 2 inches (5 centimeters) shorter than the length of the sausage. Put in the freezer for 30 minutes to set.

Mix the breakfast sausage and the Italian sausage together, put mixture into a gallon-sized bag and flatten out until the mixture reaches all sides of the bag and is equal thickness throughout (about ½ inch [13 millimeters] thick). Take out of the bag and place on a sheet of aluminum foil; spray the foil with non-stick cooking spray.

Remove the muffin mixture from freezer and place it onto the sausage. Roll the entire thing into a log, making sure to seal ends completely.

Take the bacon and weave into a checkerboard pattern. Place the sausage log onto the bacon weave and roll weave all the way around the log and season with dry rub.

Place sausage fatty onto the grate of a preheated grill/smoker at 275–300°F (135–149°C) and cook for about 2–2½ hours. You can add any kind of smoke wood you like—I like apple or sugar maple. During the last half hour, brush on BBQ sauce.

Take the fatty off the cooker and let it rest for about 30 minutes. Slice into 1–1½-inch (2.5–4-centimeter) slices, serve and enjoy.

BREAKFAST SAUSAGE FATTY

This is a take on the traditional fatty, inspired by my favorite breakfast items. It has hash browns, cheese and scrambled eggs inside breakfast sausage, all wrapped in bacon!

YIELD: 6–10 SERVINGS ★ COOK TIME: APPROXIMATELY 2½ HOURS

1 pound (455 g) breakfast sausage

1 cup (95 g) hash browns, cooked

4 tsp (20 ml) hot sauce

1 tsp (5 g) salt

½ tsp black pepper or favorite seasoning

4 eggs, scrambled

4 ounces (115 g) cheddar jack or cheddar cheese

1 pound (455 g) bacon

¼ cup (60 ml) maple syrup

2 chunks each apple and sugar maple wood

HD aluminum foil

Cooking spray

For this recipe you will be cooking on the upper end of the low and slow spectrum, somewhere around 275°F (135°C). Fill the water pan about three-quarters full with warm water. Add your smoke wood about 5 minutes before putting the fatty on.

Place the breakfast sausage into a gallon-sized bag and flatten out until the mixture reaches all sides of the bag and is equal thickness throughout (about ½ inch [13 millimeters] thick). Take out of the bag and place on a sheet of aluminum foil; spray the foil with non-stick cooking spray. Then top the sausage with hash browns and hot sauce, season with salt and pepper. Next, add the scrambled eggs and add some more hot sauce. Then top it with the cheese.

Roll the sausage up to form a giant meat log. Weave the bacon into a tight weave. Top the bacon weave with a drizzle of maple syrup and then roll it around the meat log. Set up your WSM to cook at approximately 275°F (135°C). Place the fatty on the WSM for 2–2½ hours or until the internal temperature is 165°F (74°C). During the last half hour, brush with maple syrup. Remove from the grill and let it rest covered for about 30 minutes. Slice and enjoy.

STUFFED SAUSAGE FATTY

The sausage fatty has become one of the more popular things to cook at a barbecue contest. For one, they're pretty simple to make; and two, they are just plain delicious. There are many variations, and that's part of why a fatty is so much fun to make. This is a rich and savory version that is one of my favorites.

YIELD: ABOUT 12 SERVINGS ★ COOK TIME: APPROXIMATELY 2½ HOURS

1 pound (455 g) of breakfast sausage (Jimmy Dean)
1 pound (455 g) sweet Italian sausage
¼ cup (80 g) apple butter
Smokin' Hoggz All-Purpose Rub (page 35)
8–10 slices of prosciutto
1 (8 ounce [230 g]) package cream cheese
Salt and pepper to taste
¼–½ sweet onion, diced
1 apple or pear, diced
1 pound (455 g) sliced bacon
BBQ Sauce (page 23)

For this recipe you will be cooking on the upper end of the low and slow spectrum, somewhere around 275°F (135°C). Fill the water pan about three-quarters full with warm water. Add your smoke wood about 5 minutes before putting the fatty on.

Mix the breakfast sausage and the Italian sausage together with some of the apple butter. Put the mixture into a gallon-sized bag and flatten out until the mixture reaches all sides of the bag and is equal thickness throughout (about ½ inch [13 millimeters] thick). Take out of the bag and place on a sheet of aluminum foil; spray the foil with non-stick cooking spray.

Season with the dry rub, and lay the slices of prosciutto onto the sausage mixture. Spread cream cheese on top of the prosciutto and season with some dry rub or salt and pepper.

In a skillet with some olive oil, cook up the onions for about 5 minutes on medium heat. Then add the apple/pear along with some more apple butter and cook for another 5 minutes; add salt and pepper to taste. Take off the heat and let cool.

Take cooled onion/apple mixture and spread on top of cream cheese, and add some more apple butter. Roll the entire thing into a log and completely season the outside with dry rub. Take the bacon and make a bacon weave; place the sausage log onto the bacon weave and roll weave all the way around the log and season with more dry rub.

Place the sausage fatty onto the grate of a preheated grill/smoker at 275°F (135°C) and cook for about 2–2½ hours. You can add any kind of smoke wood you like—I like apple or sugar maple. During the last half hour, brush on the BBQ sauce.

Take the fatty off the cooker and let rest for about one hour. Slice into 1–1½-inch (2.5–4-centimeter) slices. Serve and enjoy.

BABY BACK RIBS

When you think all-American BBQ, what do think of? My first thought is baby back ribs. This is what got me started in the fun and crazy world of competition BBQ. I love ribs!! I used to order them every chance I got when we would go out for dinner. Then one day I thought hmm … I bet I could make these at home. So, I went out and got a smoker. It was a small red Brinkman, and the temperature gauge read low, ideal and hot—I'm sure some of you know exactly what I'm talking about. The first set of ribs I cooked came out awful. I think there were only two bones from each rack that were even edible. It was a complete disaster! That was over 15 years ago. I have honed my barbecue skills since then, and have come up with a rib recipe that I can certainly be proud of! I think you'll like it, too!

YIELD: ABOUT 8 SERVINGS ★ COOK TIME: APPROXIMATELY 3½ HOURS

---

2 racks of loin back ribs (baby back) with the membrane from the back side of the ribs removed

½ cup (65 g) yellow mustard

½ cup (170 g) honey

½ cup (100 g) brown sugar

1 stick of butter

1 cup apple wood chips or 2–3 chunks (if using chips, soak in water for about an hour)

DRY RUB

½ cup (100 g) sugar

½ cup (120 g) kosher salt

¼ cup (50 g) brown sugar, dried

2 tbsp (4 g) chili powder

1 tbsp (7 g) ground cumin

2 tsp (5 g) accent (MSG)

2 tsp (4 g) cayenne pepper

2 tsp (5 g) black pepper, freshly ground

2 tsp (7 g) granulated garlic

2 tsp (5 g) onion powder

BBQ SAUCE

1 cup (240 g) Sweet Baby Ray's

¼ cup (60 ml) cider vinegar

¼ cup (60 ml) apple juice

2 tbsp (30 g) dry rub

First, to make the dry rub, mix all ingredients together and set aside. Same for the BBQ sauce. Next, apply some of the yellow mustard to both sides of the ribs—just enough to lightly coat them (the purpose of the mustard is to give the rub something to stick to). Then sprinkle meat with the rub and let sit for about an hour before cooking to allow meat to come to room temperature. A good overall dusting on both sides of the ribs is all you will need.

While the ribs are resting, prepare your smoker for low and slow cooking (approximately 250°F [121°C]). Fill your water pan about three-quarters full with hot water. Add your smoke wood about 5 minutes before putting the ribs on the WSM.

Now it's time to put the ribs on the cooker; you will want to put them in meat side up. Let them cook for about 2½ hours. After the 2½ hours are up, take a couple of sheets of aluminum foil and drizzle on some honey and brown sugar and a little bit of butter. Place the ribs on the honey and brown sugar meat side down. On the back side of the ribs pour some of the BBQ sauce; wrap tightly and place back on to the cooker for another hour or until done. You will know they are done when you can see the meat shrink from the bone about ½–¾ inch (13–20 millimeters). Take the ribs out of the foil and glaze them with the left over juices and let them rest for about 20 minutes. Cut them up and serve.

➺ **Some cooks like to spray ribs with a fruit juice mixture during the cooking process. Typically, this helps add some nice color, a little bit of flavor and some moisture. You could try a 50/50 mix of apple juice and cider vinegar.**

BEEF RIBS

Beef back ribs are the equivalent to the loin back (or baby back) ribs on a pig. Because they're from a cow (and not from a pig), they're much larger in size than pork ribs. The best part of the cow, the rib roast, sits right on top of the beef back ribs, so you know these are going to be tender and delicious—but only if they're prepped and cooked properly. In this recipe, I'll show you how to make excellent beef ribs each and every time!

YIELD: 8 SERVINGS ★ COOK TIME: APPROXIMATELY 4–6 HOURS

2 racks of meaty beef back ribs (about 7–8 bones per rack)
12 ounces (355 ml) lager beer

DRY RUB
3 tbsp (45 g) kosher salt
3 tbsp (24 g) chili powder
1 tbsp (7 g) coarse black pepper
2 tsp (7 g) garlic powder
2 tsp (4 g) oregano
1 tsp (2 g) cayenne pepper
1 tsp (2 g) cumin

HD aluminum foil
4 chunks of cherry and oak wood (two each)

Fire up your WSM for low and slow cooking (approximately 250–275°F [121–135°C]).

Take the ribs and remove the membrane from the bone side of each rack. The easiest way to do this is with a butter knife and a dry paper towel. Take the knife and go between the membrane and the bone and start to peel away—take the paper towel and grab onto the membrane and pull it off.

Mix all the dry rub ingredients together in a bowl.

Now season both sides of the ribs, putting more of the rub onto the meat side of the ribs.

Place onto the top rack of the WSM and cook for about 4–6 hours or until probe tender (where you stick a probe in and it feels like its going through room temperature butter).

About half way through the cook, you can spray the ribs with some of the beer, for a little added flavor.

When the ribs are done, remove them from the WSM and loosely wrap with HD foil (so steam can escape) and rest for about 15–20 minutes. Cut and serve.

CHICKEN BRINE

Brine is a salty solution that not only adds flavor to meat, it also helps keep the meat tender and moist. When you place meat into a brine, the meat draws in the salty solution, along with any other flavors you include in the brine. Because brined meat is loaded with extra liquid, it will retain more moisture as it cooks, making for a more delicious piece of meat. When you cook chicken on a smoker, either low and slow or hot and fast, you run the risk of it drying out—and nobody likes dried out chicken. If you want perfect, juicy, tender chicken every time, I highly recommend brining your chicken. This recipe will do just that!

YIELD: 5 QUARTS (5 LITERS) ★ COOK TIME: 15 MINUTES

1 cup (240 ml) boiling water
¾ cup (180 g) coarse kosher salt
¾ cup (150 g) brown sugar
1 cup (240 ml) cider vinegar
½ gallon (2 L) cold water
½ gallon (2 L) apple cider
1 tbsp (9 g) cracked black peppercorns

Take the boiling water and dissolve the salt and brown sugar. Add the rest of the ingredients and store in the fridge until ready to use.

BEER CAN CHICKEN

Beer can chicken is one of my favorite ways to cook chicken on my smoker. Not only does it look cool, it tastes even better! While the chicken is dry roasting on the outside, the inside is being bathed with steamy beer, keeping the chicken meat wonderfully moist. The result is tender, falling-off-the-bone meat, encased in salty, flavorful, crispy skin—yum!

YIELD: 4 SERVINGS ★ COOK TIME: APPROXIMATELY 2–3 HOURS

1 whole chicken (5–6 pounds [2.25–2.75 kg])

1 can (12 ounces [355 ml]) of your favorite beer

3 cloves garlic, minced

Smokin' Hoggz All-Purpose Rub (page 35)

2–3 chunks apple wood

Heat your WSM for low and slow cooking (approximately 275°F [135°C]). Fill the water pan about three-quarters full with hot water, and add the smoke wood about 5 minutes before putting the chicken on the WSM.

Clean chicken thoroughly, inside and out. Remove any unwanted parts.

Open the beer can and consume half of the beer (you don't want to waste it), and add garlic to the remaining beer.

Slide the chicken onto the can of beer, legs pointing down, so that the can supports the chicken upright (like a tripod). Generously apply the rub. Place the can with the chicken on the bottom cooking grate (the chicken may be too tall for the top grate).

Smoke chicken until cooked through. I recommend using an instant-read thermometer inserted into the thickest part of the thigh. When it registers 175°F (80°C) or 165°F (74°C) in the breast (roughly 2–3 hours), your chicken is done. You can tell it's done when you see clear liquid coming out of where you probed it.

Let chicken rest 10 minutes before carving.

APPLE WOOD SMOKED CHICKEN SALAD

I came up with this recipe after camping with some friends. We had just cooked and eaten some whole chickens, and were wondering what to do with the leftovers. So, I thought, "How about we make some chicken salad and have sandwiches?" OK, sounds interesting, right? It was just chicken, a little bit of mayo and some salt and pepper. Though it was very simple, it was delicious. Since then I have added a few more ingredients, like onions, cranberries and walnuts, to bring this dish over the top. Go ahead and give it a try, I think you'll love it!

YIELD: ABOUT 8 SERVINGS ★ COOK TIME: APPROXIMATELY 3 HOURS

1 chicken (5–6 pounds [2.25–2.75 kg])
Chicken Brine (page 69)
Olive oil
Salt and pepper
1 cup (240 g) mayonnaise
½ sweet onion, finely diced
¼ cup (40 g) dried cranberries
¼ cup (25 g) shelled and chopped walnuts
1 tbsp (8 g) chili powder
6 potato sandwich rolls

2 chunks apple wood

Set up the WSM for low and slow cooking, and fill the water pan about half way with hot water. Add the smoke wood about 5 minutes before putting the chicken on.

Brine the chicken for about 4 hours (can go up to 12 hours), remove from brine, rinse off and pat dry. (Brining the chicken will help retain moisture and also add some flavor.)

Rub the olive oil all over the chicken and season with salt and pepper.

Put the bird on the top rack of the WSM. Set it up like a tripod, resting on the two legs and the butt of the chicken. Cook for about 3 hours or until the breast (white meat) reads 165°F (74°C) and the thigh (dark meat) reads 185°F (85°C). Remove from the cooker and let rest for about 30 minutes.

Shred the chicken and mix with mayo, onion, cranberries, walnuts and chili powder.

Add salt and pepper to taste.

SPINACH AND GOAT CHEESE STUFFED CHICKEN BREAST

This is a pretty simple dish that is super rich in flavor! The tanginess of the goat cheese, slightly sweet flavor of the balsamic and the little bit of salty from the prosciutto really brings this all together for one great meal.

YIELD: 4 SERVINGS ★ COOK TIME: APPROXIMATELY 45 MINUTES

---

4 chicken breasts

4 slices prosciutto

2 cups (360 g) cooked spinach

1 cup (150 g) crumbled goat cheese

4 cloves garlic, minced

Salt and pepper

1 cup (240 ml) balsamic vinegar, reduced to ¼ cup (60 ml)

Butcher's string

2 chunks of apple wood

Fire up your WSM for low and slow cooking (about 250°F [121°C]), fill water pan about halfway with hot water and add smoke wood about 5 minutes before putting the chicken on.

Loosely wrap each chicken breast in plastic. Take a meat mallet and pound each breast until even thickness about ½ inch (13 millimeters) thick. Season with salt and pepper. Lay the slice of prosciutto on top of the chicken, add about ½ cup (90 grams) of spinach, ¼ cup (40 grams) of goat cheese and about ¼ of the minced garlic. Roll chicken up and tie with butcher's string about every 1 inch (2.5 centimeters). Season with salt and pepper.

Place onto the top grate of the WSM, and cook until you get an internal temperature of 165°F (74°C).

Remove from cooker and let sit for 5 minutes, then serve and drizzle with balsamic reduction.

PASTRAMI, DRY CURED

I found that I could make pastrami that gave the store-bought stuff a real run for its money, and it was a fun process! If you like pastrami, and you know how to cook brisket, you might as well give this a try.

YIELD: 15 SERVINGS ★ COOK TIME: APPROXIMATELY 3+ HOURS

1 brisket flat (5–8 pounds [2.25–3.75 kg])

DRY CURE

¼ cup (60 g) Morton Tender Quick
¼ cup (50 g) brown sugar (light or dark)
¼ cup (30 g) coarse ground black pepper
2 tbsp (20 g) garlic
2 tbsp (14 g) ground coriander
2 tbsp (13 g) ground mustard seed

COOKING RUB

4 tbsp (30 g) coarse black pepper
1 tsp (3 g) garlic powder
1 tsp (2 g) onion powder
1 tsp (2 g) ground coriander
1 tsp (2 g) paprika
1 tsp (2 g) ground mustard seed

3 chunks of cherry wood
Baking pan
Wire rack
Resealable bag or zippered storage bag

Make the cure and the rub by mixing the ingredients into two small bowls. Set aside.

Trim the fat from the brisket flat to about ⅛ inch (3 millimeters) (this will allow the cure to penetrate down into the meat). Season both sides of the brisket with the dry cure rub and place the meat into a resealable bag. Apply any remaining rub onto the nonfat side of the brisket. Put the bag onto a sheet pan and place in the fridge for 3 to 4 days (depending on when you will be cooking), turning the bag twice a day (morning and night) to allow for maximum cure.

After the cure, remove from bag and rinse off. Soak for about an hour in cold water, changing the water at the 30-minute mark. This will help control the saltiness of the pastrami.

Fire up your WSM for low and slow cooking (approximately 250°F [121°C]), and add the smoking wood about 5 minutes before cooking.

Season the cured brisket with the cooking rub. Let the meat sit for about an hour before putting it on the WSM. Then, place it on the WSM, and cook until you get an internal temp of 190°F (88°C). Start checking around the 3-hour mark. Remove from the WSM and wrap in foil in the fridge for 12 hours.

When it is time to serve, it is time to steam heat and tenderize. You can make a steamer by putting a wire rack in a baking pan. If necessary, you can sit the wire rack on balls of foil to keep it out of the water. Unwrap the meat and put it on the foil in which it was wrapped or the steam will wash off a lot of the rub. Do not slice the meat first.

Fire up your WSM again, this time to the higher end of the low and slow range (about 275°F [135°C]).

Put the pan on the top rack of the WSM and steam it an hour or two until heated through to 203°F (95°C). The exact time will depend on the meat's thickness and how hot the water is. Add hot water as needed, making sure the pan never dries out. Don't rush this. Take it all the way to 203°F (95°C).

Now to serve this, hand slice it to about ⅛ inch (3 millimeters) and stack onto some good rye bread and add some brown spicy mustard.

MAPLE CURED PORK BELLY

If you have never had homemade bacon, you, my friend, are in for a delicious treat. Homemade bacon is probably one of the easiest things to do, and is sooooo much better and much less expensive than the store bought stuff. A 10–12 pound (4.5–5.5 kg) pork belly will run you about $3 per pound (455 g). That's about half of what you would spend on prepared bacon. I'm telling you, once you try this, you won't be buying anymore grocery store bacon again!!

YIELD: 10–12 POUNDS (4.5–5.5 KG) ★ COOK TIME: APPROXIMATELY 3 HOURS

12 pounds (5.5 kg) pork belly, skin off
1 cup (240 g) kosher salt
1 cup (200 g) brown sugar
1 cup (240 ml) real maple syrup
3 tsp (15 g) pink salt (curing salt)

3–4 chunks sugar maple smoking wood

Mix together the salts, sugar and syrup—this will turn into a paste.

Put pork belly in a 2½-gallon (9.5 liter) zippered storage bag. With the fat side up, apply some of the paste; rub it all over the fat side. Turn over and apply the remaining paste and rub it all over the meat side. Seal the bag and put it into a full pan and put it in the refrigerator. This will be there for about 6 to 7 days, turn over once a day. After 7 days, remove and rinse off with cold water. Slice off a small piece and cook; if it is too salty, soak in water for an hour, and repeat. After it has been rinsed and soaked, dry it off and put it back into the pan fat side facing down and put back into refrigerator overnight. This process will allow the surface of the meat to form a thin coating called a pellicle, which will allow the smoke to stick to the meat a little better.

Go ahead and fire up the WSM for low and slow cooking (approximately 200–225°F [93–107°C]). This will be a short cook so you don't need to fill the charcoal pan all the way. Fill the water pan up about halfway with cold water. Add the smoke wood about 5 minutes before putting the meat on the smoker. You will want to cook this at about 200°F (93°C) until the internal temperature reaches 150°F (66°C), approximately 3 hours.

Remove and let it cool. Store in the fridge until ready to eat, but I know that will hard to do, it is bacon!!! Cut yourself off a piece and cook it up, and go to your happy place!!!

POT ROAST

Pot roast was a standard meal when I was growing up, and it continues to be in my parents' household. Pot roast requires slow cooking over low heat to ensure tender, flavorful meat. Pot roasts typically use the tougher cuts of beef—a chuck roast or shoulder roast—which are loaded with flavor. Slow cooking at low heat is what melts the tough connective tissue between the muscle fibers, leaving you with tender meat that flakes apart from your fork.

YIELD: 6 SERVINGS ★ COOK TIME: APPROXIMATELY 5–6 HOURS

---

6 pounds (2.75 kg) bone-in chuck roast

Olive oil

Salt and pepper

Garlic powder

1 packet of gravy mix

1 cup (240 ml) beef stock

2 tbsp (25 g) butter

4 medium potatoes cut into 1" (2.5 cm) chunks

4 carrots peeled and sliced 1" (2.5 cm) thick

1 large sweet onion cut into quarters

Disposable aluminum half pan

HD aluminum foil

Fat separator

4 chunks of hickory wood

Fire up the WSM for low and slow cooking to (approximately 250°F [121°C]). Fill the water pan with hot water, and put the wood chunks in about 10 minutes before putting the meat on. Adjust the bottom vents as needed throughout the cook to maintain 250°F (121°C).

Coat the chuck roast with olive oil and liberally season with salt, pepper and garlic powder. Let the roast sit out for about an hour before going on the WSM.

Place the roast into an aluminum half pan, sprinkle with gravy mix and pour beef stock over roast. Place onto the top rack of the WSM and cook uncovered for about 2 hours, then cover with HD foil and continue to cook for about 5–6 more hours until fall-off-the-bone tender. With about 2 hours left in the cook, add the butter, potatoes, carrots and onion. You can check the tenderness of the roast by poking it with a fork; it should go in with little resistance and when you twist the fork the meat should start to shred and pull clean from the bone. Be sure to keep an eye on the water pan after about 3–4 hours and add hot water if needed.

Remove from the WSM and let rest covered for about 15–20 minutes.

Pour liquid in to the fat separator and use as an au jus. Serve with veggies.

PULLED PORK WITH ROOT BEER BBQ SAUCE

Pulled pork is my favorite BBQ of all time, everywhere I go, whether it is passing by a roadside stand or walking around at a BBQ contest, I always try the pulled pork. I was at a fair a few years ago and saw someone selling pulled pork sandwiches with a root beer sauce, so I just had to try it. Awesome to say the least. After a few tries at it, I think I finally have something to be proud of. Here is my version.

YIELD: ABOUT 12–15 SERVINGS ★ COOK TIME: APPROXIMATELY 6–8 HOURS

1 Boston butt (8–10 pounds [3.75–4.5 kg])
Salt and pepper
1 bottle of Stubb's Pork Marinade
12–15 bulky rolls

ROOT BEER BBQ SAUCE
1 bottle root beer (2 L)
1½ cups (355 ml) apple cider vinegar
½ cup (120 g) ketchup
½ cup (125 g) yellow mustard
2 tbsp (30 ml) lemon juice
2 tbsp (35 g) Worcestershire sauce
1 tbsp (15 ml) Tabasco
1 tsp (5 g) kosher salt
1 tsp (2g) black pepper
2 tbsp (25 g) cold unsalted butter

On this recipe you'll be cooking around 250°F (121°C). So fire up your WSM for low and slow cooking, and fill the water pan with hot water almost to the top of the pan. Add your smoke wood when you put the butt on the cooker.

Season the pork butt with salt and pepper. Place the pork butt, fat side up, on the top rack. Season the fat side also with salt and pepper.

Cook until the internal temperature reaches between 160–165°F (71–74°C). This should take 6–8 hours. Remove from the WSM and wrap in foil fat side down and add the bottle of Stubb's Pork Marinade. Put the pork back on the WSM and continue cooking until internal temp of 195–205°F (91–96°C)—start checking temp of the butt after 1½–2 hours. Remove butt from the WSM, open foil and steam down for 10 minutes (until you cannot see steam coming from the foil).

Wrap butt in a towel and let rest for about 1–2 hours in a dry cooler. Take butt out of foil and with two forks, pull apart the meat into small chunks. Toss with the root beer BBQ sauce and serve on fresh bulky rolls.

To make the BBQ sauce, reduce the root beer to 1 cup (240 milliliters) over medium heat in a large saucepan—this takes about an hour. Add the apple cider vinegar, ketchup, yellow mustard, lemon juice, Worcestershire sauce, Tabasco, salt and pepper. Stir well and simmer for 20 minutes. Finish the sauce by whisking in the cold butter for extra body and flavor.

SHREDDED BBQ BEEF

This is another fan favorite when watching football games up here in New England. The great thing about this one is you can cook it the day before and just heat it up on the grill while you're tailgating.

YIELD: 10–12 SERVINGS ★ COOK TIME: APPROXIMATELY 2–3 HOURS

BEEF RUB
2 tbsp (30 g) kosher salt
2 tbsp (14 g) black pepper
2 tbsp (16 g) chili powder
2 tsp (4 g) cayenne pepper

5–6 pounds (2.25–2.75 kg) chuck eye roast
Olive oil
12 potato rolls
BBQ Sauce (page 23)

Disposable aluminum half pan

First, to make the rub, mix all ingredients in an airtight container and store until ready to use.

Fire up the WSM for low and slow cooking (approximately 250°F [121°C]). Fill the charcoal chamber about halfway full with unlit charcoal briquettes and then spread about 30 hot coals over the unlit ones.

Cut the roast into quarters. This helps the meat cook faster and creates more surface area for dark, smoky outside meat to form during cooking. Remove any gristle or large areas of fat. Rub the olive oil over all 4 pieces and coat each piece with rub.

Place 2 fist-sized chunks of smoke wood on the hot coals. I like apple wood and hickory. Assemble the cooker with the water pan in place and fill it with cool water. Place the 4 pieces of chuck eye in a foil pan on the top cooking grate. Arrange them to maximize their exposure to the smoke and so they don't touch one another.

Set the top vent to 100 percent open and keep it that way throughout the entire cooking process. Start with all 3 bottom vents 100 percent open. As the cooker approaches 200°F (93°C), begin to partially close all 3 bottom vents so the cooker temperature does not exceed 250°F (121°C). Adjust the bottom vents as needed to maintain this temperature range throughout the cooking process.

After 3 hours cover with foil and cook for another 2–3 hours.

Remove the meat from the smoker and let rest for 30 minutes. Pour off the juices into a fat separator. Reserve ¼ to ½ cup (60 to 120 milliliters) of the juices for later.

Shred the meat using forks or just your fingers. Mix ½ cup (120 grams) of BBQ sauce and add about ¼ cup (60 milliliters) of reserved juices. Mix the sauce into the shredded beef. Serve on the potato rolls.

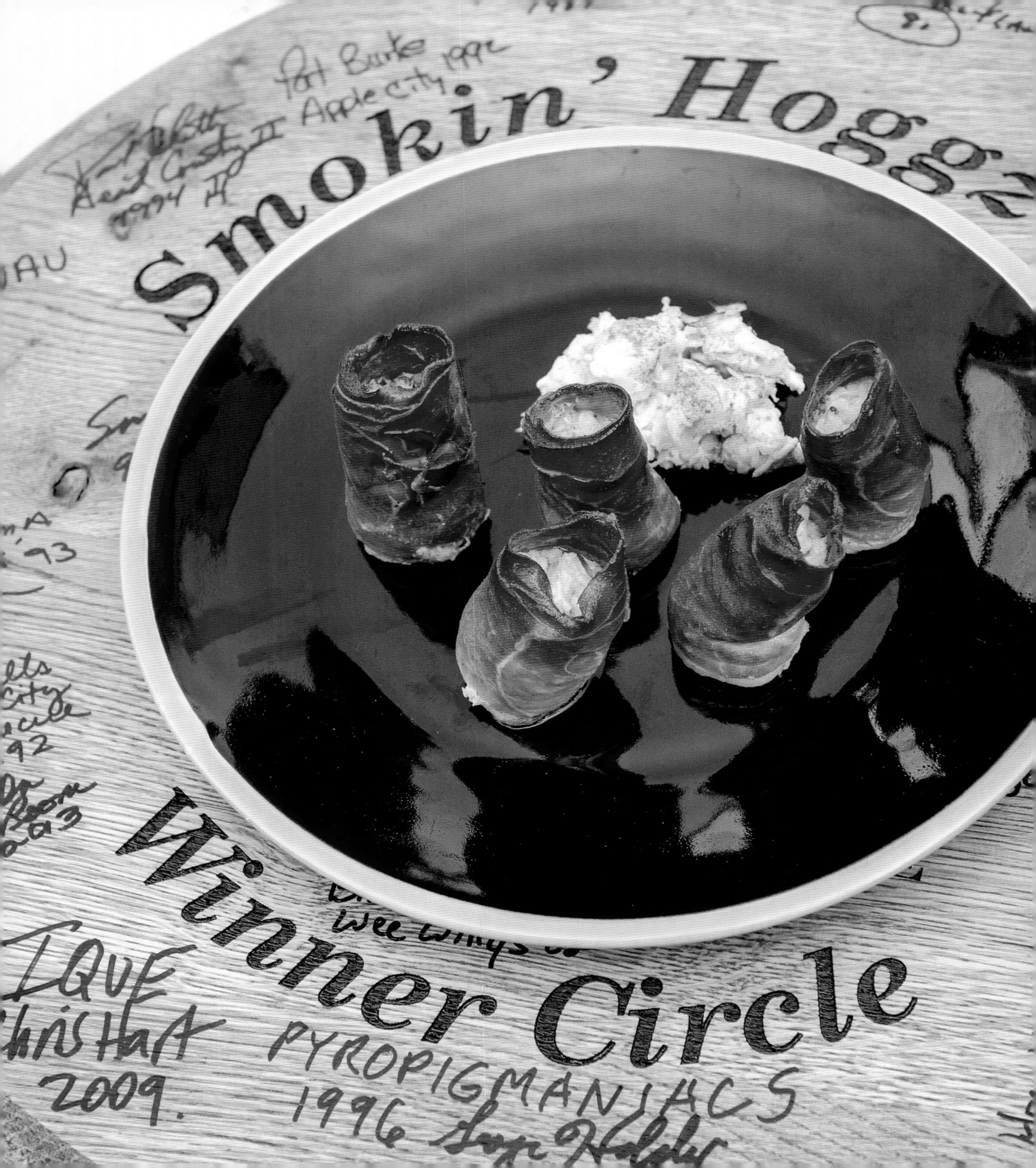
Smokin' Hoggz
Winner Circle
PYROPIGMANIACS
1996
2009.

SMOKED SEA SCALLOPS WRAPPED IN PROSCIUTTO

Scallops are fantastic, especially when fresh. We have a fish guy we go to during the summer where we can get fresh scallops caught that morning. These little babies are wonderful. They are so light and have such a beautiful, sweet taste to them! If you really want to impress a lot of people at your next party, then you have to make this recipe!!!

YIELD: 4 SERVINGS ★ COOK TIME: APPROXIMATELY 45 MINUTES

12 large sea scallops
2 tsp (10 g) kosher salt
2 tsp (5 g) black pepper
2 tsp (5 g) sweet Hungarian paprika
12 slices prosciutto
1 cup (135 g) fresh lump crab meat
1 stick of unsalted butter, cut into 12 equal slices
2 tbsp (5 g) fresh parsley, finely chopped

2 chunks alder wood
12 toothpicks

Set up your WSM for low and slow cooking (approximately 250°F [121°C]), and fill your water pan about halfway with hot water. Add you smoke wood about 5 minutes before putting the scallops on the cooker. Remember this is a short cook, so you won't need to use a lot of charcoal.

First, wash and clean the scallops in cold water and pat dry with a paper towel. Usually there is a small muscle on the side of the scallop—you want to make sure to remove it. You won't need a knife; it should just come off using your fingers.

Season the scallops with salt, pepper and paprika.

Wrap each scallop with a piece of prosciutto, making sure it sticks up over the top of the scallop by about a ¼–½ inch (6–13 millimeters). Secure each with a toothpick.

Take about a spoonful of the crab and place it on top of the scallop, then place a slice of butter on top of that. Season with a little more black pepper.

Place on to the top grate of the WSM and cook for about 45 minutes.

Remove from smoker, take the toothpick out, garnish with a little sprinkle of parsley and serve immediately.

AWARD-WINNING SALMON

This recipe is very special to me. I developed this recipe before I even thought about competing. Turns out, this is also the first recipe I ever turned in during a competition. The first time I used it, it received fourth place. Since then, this recipe has won several first-place calls in various competitions.

YIELD: 4 SERVINGS ★ COOK TIME: 20–30 MINUTES

---

2 pounds (910 g) salmon
¼ cup (60 ml) real maple syrup
¼ cup (50 g) brown sugar
Smokin' Hoggz All-Purpose Rub (page 35)

2 chunks of alder wood

Cut the salmon into four 8-ounce (230 gram) servings, leaving the skin on. Apply the maple syrup all over each piece. Sprinkle the rub on all three sides, apply a good amount of the brown sugar and let sit in a container in the fridge for about an hour.

While you're waiting for the salmon to set up, prepare your WSM for the upper end of the low and slow style (about 275°F [135°C]). For salmon, I like to use woods like alder, or any fruitwood will work just fine. Add the wood about 5 minutes before putting the salmon on the cooker.

Place salmon on the top grate of the WSM, and cook until it reaches an internal temperature of 135°F (57°C) (medium). If you like your salmon cooked a little more, go until the internal temperature reaches 145°F (63°C). Remove from the WSM and let rest for 5 minutes.

THANKSGIVING TURKEY, BUTTERFLIED

This is my favorite way to prepare a Thanksgiving turkey. The reason I like to butterfly a turkey is that you end up with a more even cook of both the white and dark meat. It's a pretty cool presentation, and it's a lot easier to carve up. So you think bringing a turkey to the family gathering seems like a lot of work? It's really not. It just takes a little extra time—but the results are simply awesome. No more dry, overcooked bird for your holidays!

COOK TIME: ABOUT 3 HOURS

1 fresh turkey (15 pounds [7 kg])
Turkey Brine (page 90)
2 cups (475 ml) Butter Injection (page 90)
Fresh ground pepper
Olive oil

Butcher's string
Full-size aluminum disposable pan
Meat injector
5 gallon (20 L) food-grade bucket (empty and clean) or a dry empty cooler
3 chunks apple wood

This is going to be a two-day process, but it is so worth it!!

Prepare the turkey by taking it out of the packaging and removing the bag of giblets (save for later for giblet gravy). Remove any excess skin around each opening and rinse off.

Place the turkey in an empty 5 gallon (20 liter) food-grade bucket breast side down and add the brine. Place in the fridge overnight. If you don't have a bucket, you can use a dry, empty cooler and an extra-large zippered storage bag. Place the turkey in the bag breast side down and place inside the cooler. Add the brine, remove air and then seal the bag. Fill the rest of the cooler with ice and brine overnight.

Remove turkey from the brine, rinse off and pat dry. Place turkey into a full-size aluminum pan, and put back in the fridge overnight to let skin dry out. This will help to create that crispy skin everyone loves.

At this time go ahead and set up the WSM for the upper end of low and slow cooking (approximately 275°F [135°C]). Fill the water pan about two-thirds full of hot water. About 15 minutes before putting the bird on the WSM, add your smoke wood.

Now for the fun part!! You'll need a pair of really good poultry shears or kitchen shears for removing the backbone. Cut through the bones on each side of the backbone, staying as close to the backbone as possible. With the backbone removed, flip the turkey over and press down hard with both hands to crack and flatten the breastbone. Fold the wings under the turkey so they won't burn during cooking. Tie the legs together using butcher's string.

Take the meat injector and inject the butter injection throughout the breast, legs and thighs. Brush the turkey all over with a very thin layer of olive oil and sprinkle with fresh cracked pepper.

Place on the top rack of the WSM, and cook until the internal temperature of the breast (white meat) is 165°F (74°C) and the thigh (dark meat) is 175°F (80°C).

Remove and let rest about 30 minutes uncovered. Carve it up and serve.

 (continued)

➜ Prepping to remove backbone

➜ Cutting out backbone

➜ Removing backbone

➜ Prepping butter injection

➻ Injecting breast

➻ Injecting thigh

➻ Injecting leg

➻ Almost ready to come off

BUTTER INJECTION

We all know turkey can sometimes be a little dry and kind of bland in taste. Well, this injection is sure to make your next turkey super moist and flavorful.

YIELD: ABOUT 2¾ CUPS (650 ML)

1 stick butter
2 cups (475 ml) chicken broth
¼ cup (60 ml) lemon juice
2 tsp (7 g) garlic powder
2 tsp (5 g) onion powder
2 tsp (5 g) finely ground pepper
1 tsp (2 g) ground thyme

Melt the butter in a small saucepan. Add the remaining ingredients and mix well. Allow mixture to cool enough to work with and load into a meat injector—refrigerate if necessary.

TURKEY BRINE

One of the best things you can do to improve the flavor and moisture of a turkey (or chicken) is to brine it. Brining is basically soaking the bird in a salty solution for an extended period of time. The salt actually changes the molecular structure of the meat. Now, you might think the meat would be too salty, right? Instead, it creates some of the most tender and moist meat you'll ever have.

You can buy premade brines, but what's the fun in that? Making your own brine is easy to do, plus you get to pick the ingredients so you know it'll be fresh and delicious! You will only want to brine fresh turkeys, because frozen turkeys typically have already been injected with a similar solution.

YIELD: ABOUT 2 GALLONS (7.5 L)

1 gallon (4 L) heavily iced spring water (saved for later)
½ gallon (2 L) apple cider
1 quart (950 ml) chicken stock
1 quart (950 ml) spring water
1½ cups (365 g) kosher salt
1 cup (200 g) dark brown sugar, packed
1 cup (240 ml) cider vinegar
1 cinnamon stick
3 whole orange peels
4 cloves garlic, chopped
¼ cup (35 g) mixed peppercorns
3 tbsp (5 g) rosemary leaves
1 tbsp (10 g) allspice berries

Combine all of the ingredients in a large stockpot and stir until salt and sugar have dissolved. Bring to a boil and turn off heat. Add the gallon of ice-cold water. Store in the fridge until ready for use.

PIG CANDY

All right, if you've never made or tasted pig candy, strap yourself in for a seriously heavenly indulgence. After having some of these wonderful, sweet, swinetastic eats, you will be dancing around like a little kid on Christmas morning!!!

YIELD: 8 SERVINGS ★ COOK TIME: APPROXIMATELY 1–1½ HOURS

---

1 pound (455 g) thick-cut bacon (or see page 77 for how to make your own bacon)

¼–½ cup (60–120 ml) pure maple syrup

½ tsp (2 g) chili powder (Any kind of chili powder will work for this recipe, for a mild chili try ancho. If you like it spicier try chipotle or cayenne.)

½–1 cup (100–200 g) dark brown sugar (more as needed)

HD aluminum foil
Cooking spray
2 chunks sugar maple wood

Set up the WSM for low and slow cooking (approximately 250–275°F [121–135°C]), and add wood chunks about 5 minutes before the bacon goes on.

Place the foil onto the top grate of the WSM and spray with cooking spray. Lay out bacon pieces next to each other, and drizzle each piece with maple syrup. Lightly sprinkle on chili powder (you don't need a lot, this is more for a little back end heat/flavor), and liberally sprinkle brown sugar onto each piece.

Place on the top section of WSM and cook for about 1–1½ hours or until bacon reaches your desired doneness.

CHAPTER TWO

THE SECRETS TO HOT *and* FAST COOKING ON THE WSM AND OTHER SMOKERS

As the name implies, the hot and fast cooking method uses a hotter temperature and shorter cooking time than the low and slow method associated with traditional barbecue. As part of your development as a backyard cook, we think it's a good idea to learn the hot and fast method. For beginners, the recipes in this section use all the same basic cooking skills that you will use when making traditional low and slow barbecue. In this sense, they're not only great practice, but you'll also obtain a finished product in much less time than if you used the low and slow method. For experienced cooks, the hot and fast method is a great fallback when life's sudden intricacies flare up and you unexpectedly find you're pressed for time—before you've even started cooking.

When you cook using the hot and fast method, try to light enough charcoal so that it lasts throughout the entire cooking process. We recommend using lump charcoal, as it burns hotter and is more suited to this style of cooking.

ADVANTAGES OF THE HOT AND FAST METHOD:

★ Shorter cooking durations that generally last 4 to 6 hours
★ Typically does not require additional charcoal during the cook time
★ Favored when you prefer that charcoal be fully lit during cooking process

THINGS TO KEEP IN MIND:

★ If the WSM runs too hot, bringing the temperature down can be problematic
★ Ideal temperature range is 325–375°F (163–190°C)

BASIC WORKFLOW TWEAKS FOR HOT AND FAST METHOD:

1. Fully open the top and bottom vents. This configuration will help channel a significant amount of air throughout the entire cooking process, allowing the WSM to maintain a high cooking temperature.

2. Dump one chimney of unlit charcoal inside the charcoal ring.

3. Light one full chimney of charcoal. Wait for the charcoal at the top of the chimney to begin to turn gray or until you see flames rising out of the top of the chimney.

4. Using heat-resistant gloves, dump the hot charcoal into the charcoal ring.

5. Cover the top of the water pan with aluminum foil to catch grease and prevent it from burning. (DO NOT fill the water pan with water.)

6. Assemble the WSM, and then place the lid on top.

7. Let the WSM come up to temperature (approximately 325–375°F [163–190°C]). This typically takes 30 to 60 minutes.

8. After the temperature stabilizes, add your smoke wood and place the meat on the cooking grates.

➻ **If you are having trouble bringing the temperature up, open the side access door to let more oxygen reach the hot charcoal. More oxygen reaching the hot coals will help raise the temperature.**

HIGH HEAT BRISKET

When I first started cooking at barbecue contests, I learned how to cook brisket using the hot and fast method. I had done a couple using the traditional low and slow method, but couldn't quite get the consistency I liked until I started using the hot and fast method. This is a great method for cooking briskets, not only because it takes less time, but also because the results are fantastic each and every time.

YIELD: 20–30 SERVINGS ★ COOK TIME: APPROXIMATELY 4½ HOURS

BRISKET RUB

¼ cup (60 g) kosher salt
¼ cup (50 g) sugar
1 tbsp (7 g) coarse black pepper
1 tbsp (10 g) garlic powder
1 tbsp (7 g) onion powder
2 tbsp (20 g) chili powder
2 tsp (4 g) cayenne pepper

1 brisket (10–12 pounds [4.5–5.5 kg])
Brisket Injection (page 34)
Brisket Marinade (page 34)
BBQ Sauce (page 23)

2 chunks each of apple and hickory wood
HD aluminum foil

Set up your WSM for hot and fast cooking (approximately 350°F [177°C]). I like to use apple and hickory when cooking brisket hot and fast, but you can use whatever wood you like.

You will also want to line your water pan with some HD aluminum foil, this will greatly help with clean up when you are done.

Mix all the rub ingredients in a bowl.

Inject your brisket with the injection, and then apply rub liberally all over the brisket. Let it sit in the fridge for 4 hours to overnight.

Place it on the top rack of the WSM and cook for 2½ hours or until it reaches an internal temperature of 165°F (74°C).

When the desired internal temp is reached, remove the brisket from the cooker and prepare for wrapping. Lay out a sheet of HD foil large enough to completely wrap the brisket. Wrap in the foil and add heated brisket marinade, and cook for an additional 1½–2 hours until you reach an internal temp of 200°F (93°C). (Don't worry, cooking until this temperature at high won't turn you brisket mushy. Cooking at high heat allows you to cook your meat to a higher internal temperature.) Remove the brisket from the WSM and vent the foil for about 10 minutes to help stop the cooking process. Wrap it back up and set it aside in a dry empty cooler and let it rest for about an hour.

After about an hour rest time, take the brisket out of the cooler and separate the flat from the point. To do this, take a long slicing knife and place the knife between the point and flat and slice at an angle, going toward the end of the flat—it should be like slicing through warm butter. Go ahead and cube up the point into 1-inch (2.5-centimeter) pieces, place into a pan, add some BBQ sauce and put back on the cooker for an additional 30 minutes. Slice the flat into ¼-inch (6-millimeter) thick slices and put them back into the foil juice for about 10 minutes—this will help add a little flavor to this already delicious brisket.

Serve slices by themselves or with a side of beans (see page 46 for my Kicked-Up BBQ Baked Beans recipe) and coleslaw. Or you could make a delicious sandwich served on a bulky roll with a little BBQ sauce.

HIGH HEAT CHICKEN LOLLIPOPS

Meat on a stick—a dish with its own built-in utensil! These chicken lollipops are sure to be a hit at your next cookout, particularly with the kids. One look and your friends and family will think you are the next television food star!

YIELD: 12 SERVINGS ★ COOK TIME: APPROXIMATELY 1 HOUR

1½ cups (355 ml) chicken broth
1½ tsp (25 g) accent (MSG)
2 tsp (5 g) dehydrated butter powder
12 chicken drumsticks, skin on
Smokin' Hoggz Dry Rub (page 23)
1½ cups (360 g) Sweet Baby Ray's Honey Chipotle BBQ Sauce
¼ cup (85 g) honey
½ cup (120 ml) white grape juice

2–3 chunks sugar maple or apple wood

First, combine the chicken broth, accent and butter powder together, making sure accent dissolves completely; store in fridge until ready to use.

Prepare the WSM for hot and fast cooking (approximately 300–350°F [149–177°C]). Add wood chunks about 10 minutes before putting the chicken on.

With a paring knife, cut the tendons at the narrow end of each drum. Scrape the meat down as far as possible without removing the meat completely, to form a round lollipop shape. With a pair of pliers go ahead and remove all the ligaments and smaller bones and throw out.

Make sure all the meat is down to one end of the bone and be sure the skin is covering all the meat—trim excess skin if necessary.

With a meat injector, inject about ½ to 1 ounce (15 to 30 milliliters) of chicken broth mix all throughout meat.

Season drums with rub and place on the top rack of the WSM. Cook for about 1 hour or until internal temperature reaches 165°F (74°C).

In a medium saucepan, heat the barbecue sauce, honey and grape juice.

Remove drums from the smoker. Using tongs or gloved hands, submerge each drum into warm sauce. Shake off excess sauce and place back on the smoker, directly on grill grate. Cook until sauce is caramelized, about 15 minutes.

Remove drums from smoker. Let them rest for 10 minutes and serve.

HOT AND FAST PORK BUTT WITH SIMPLE MUSTARD SAUCE

This is a great recipe if you don't have all night to cook. The best part is that you don't have to get up before the birds to have this ready for dinner time!

YIELD: ABOUT 12 SERVINGS ★ COOK TIME: APPROXIMATELY 5½ HOURS

MUSTARD SAUCE
½ cup (120 g) honey mustard
½ cup (120 ml) cider vinegar
2 cups (400 g) packed light brown sugar

1 pork butt (8 pounds [3.75 kg])
Pork Injection (page 29)
Smokin' Hoggz Dry Rub (page 23)
Pork Braise (page 29)
12 deli rolls
Coleslaw, to serve

First, heat the mustard sauce ingredients in a saucepan until the brown sugar is dissolved. Remove from heat and cool in the fridge.

Set up your WSM for hot and fast cooking (approximately 350°F [177°C]). I like to use apple or sugar maple when cooking pork, but you can use whatever wood you like.

You will also want to line your water pan with some HD aluminum foil, this will greatly help with clean up when you are done.

Inject butt with the injection—you probably won't use it all, but that's ok. Apply the rub liberally all over the butt, and let sit in the fridge for 4 hours to overnight.

Place on the top rack of the WSM and cook for 3½ hours or until the butt reaches an internal temperature of about 165°F (74°C).

When the desired internal temperature is reached, remove from the cooker and prepare for wrapping. Lay out a piece of HD foil large enough to wrap entire butt.

Place butt in foil and add the pork braise. Wrap completely in foil and return to the cooker and cook for an additional 1½–2 hours until you reach an internal temp of 200–205°F (93–96°C). (Don't worry, cooking until this temperature at high won't turn your pork mushy; cooking at high heat allows you to cook your meat to a higher internal temperature.) Remove from the WSM and open (vent) the foil to help stop the cooking process. Vent the pork butt for about 10 minutes. Then wrap it back up and set it aside in a dry empty cooler and let rest for about an hour.

Shred pork and strain the juices from foil and mix back in with the pork. Serve on rolls with coleslaw and mustard sauce.

➠ **When shredding pork by hand, it's a good idea to go out and get yourself a pair of cotton gloves, then put your food-safe gloves over those. The cotton glove will allow you to shred the pork much easier without burning your hands.**

BUTTERMILK CHEDDAR BISCUITS

Biscuits are one of the all-time great Southern comfort foods. There is nothing better than taking a freshly made biscuit, cutting it open, slapping a big old glob of butter on it and drizzling on some honey.

YIELD: 8–10 SERVINGS ★ COOK TIME: APPROXIMATELY 20 MINUTES

2–2¼ cups (225 g) all-purpose flour, plus more for work surface

2¼ tsp (10 g) baking powder

¾ tsp (3 g) baking soda

½ tsp salt

¼ tsp ground pepper

6 tbsp (90 g) cold unsalted butter, cut into small pieces

¾ cup (180 ml) buttermilk

¾ cup (85 g) shredded cheddar cheese

½ tbsp (8 g) unsalted butter, melted

Fire up the WSM for hot and fast cooking (approximately 400°F [205°C]).

In a large bowl, whisk together 2 cups (200 grams) flour, baking powder, baking soda, salt and pepper. Cut in the butter with a pastry blender until the mixture resembles coarse crumbs, with some pea-size lumps. Mix in the buttermilk and cheese until combined. With a floured hand, knead dough against side of the bowl until it holds together. If it is still sticky, knead in up to ¼ cup (25 grams) more flour.

After kneading biscuit dough, pour it out onto a lightly floured work surface. Pat the dough to 1 inch (2.5 centimeter) thick. With a floured 2 inch (5 centimeter) biscuit cutter, cut out rounds as close together as possible. Place them on a baking sheet. Gather scraps, pat again and cut out more rounds.

Brush the tops with the melted butter. Cook in the WSM until biscuits are golden brown, roughly 18 to 20 minutes. Serve biscuits with some delicious sausage gravy or eggs and bacon.

SULLY'S DAMN DIP

When I first started competing, I kept hearing people talk about this amazingly delicious late-night dip served with tortilla chips. I asked what it was and wondered why it's called Damn Dip. They told me it's made by a guy named Sully, and it's the best damn dip you'll ever eat! Well, they weren't kidding. Melted cheese, chili, salsa, jalapeños, the melding of flavors was outstanding! I got hooked, and now I crave this Northeast specialty at every contest I go to. Normally this is cooked on a 22-inch (56-centimeter) charcoal grill, so I have modified the recipe and scaled it down to fit on the 18-inch (46-centimeter) WSM. Here's my take on Sully's famous Damn Dip.

YIELD: ABOUT 25 SERVINGS ★ COOK TIME: APPROXIMATELY 1½ HOURS

---

2 cans Hormel Chili Hot & Spicy with Beans

Smokin' Hoggz Dry Rub (page 23)

1 bottle Cholula Chipotle Hot Sauce

2 (8 ounce [230 g]) bars Philly Cream Cheese, cubed into ½ ounce (15 g) pieces

1 jar Mrs. Renfro's Green Salsa

1 jar Dr. Gonzo's Hot Pepper Mash

8 ounces (230 g) mozzarella/provolone cheese, shredded

8 ounces (230 g) cheddar cheese, shredded

1 bottle Cholula Chili Garlic Sauce

4 large bags of tortilla chips

Cast iron pan or HD aluminum pan

Fire up your WSM for high heat cooking (approximately 350–375°F [177–191°C]). I recommend using lump charcoal for this one, as it will burn a little hotter than the standard briquettes.

The key to this recipe is YOU ABSOLUTELY CANNOT MIX OR STIR ANY OF THE INGREDIENTS. They land where they land. Use a large cast iron pan (minimum 12 inches [31 centimeters]). If you don't have one, a HD pan will do.

For the first layer, add both cans of chili, sprinkle with dry rub and add the bottle of chipotle hot sauce. Next, add the second layer by breaking up the cream cheese and scattering it throughout. For the third layer, add Mrs. Renfro's Green Salsa and Dr. Gonzo's Hot Pepper Mash.

Then comes the fourth layer, sprinkling on the shredded cheeses. And lastly, add the remaining bottle of chili garlic sauce over the top of the cheese layer.

Put the dip onto the top grate of the WSM, and cook until bubbly around the edges—could be 1–2 hours, check it after an hour.

When done, remove and let it rest for 15 minutes. Open a bag of chips and dig in!

JALAPEÑO BACON CHEDDAR CORN BREAD

Cooked in a cast iron skillet, oh yeah! The best parts are the crispy edges of the browned up cheddar cheese and the subtle heat from the jalapeño. I think this is the perfect complement to any BBQ.

YIELD: 8 SERVINGS ★ COOK TIME: APPROXIMATELY 30 MINUTES

½ pound (230 g) bacon, cooked and crumbled (reserve the bacon)

3 cups (300 g) all-purpose flour

1 cup (170 g) yellow cornmeal

¼ cup (50 g) white sugar

2 tbsp (25 g) baking powder

2 tbsp (30 g) kosher salt

1 cup (240 ml) milk

1 cup (240 ml) buttermilk

1 cup (205 g) unsalted butter, melted

3 extra large eggs, lightly beaten

1 cup (115 g) cheddar cheese, shredded

3 jalapeño peppers, diced

Set up your WSM for high heat cooking (approximately 350°F [177°C]), and empty the water pan.

Place a skillet with bacon grease on the top rack to keep warm. Combine the flour, cornmeal, sugar, baking powder and salt in a large bowl. Whisk the milk, buttermilk, butter and eggs in another bowl; stir milk mixture into flour mixture until just combined. Batter will be slightly lumpy. Fold in cheddar cheese, jalapeño peppers and half the bacon. Allow batter to rest at room temperature for 10 minutes.

Remove skillet from the WSM and pour the batter into the hot skillet and sprinkle with other half of crumbled bacon, gently pressing bacon into batter. Place this back onto the top rack of the WSM, and cook until a toothpick inserted into the center comes out clean, about 30–35 minutes. Cool in the pan for 10 minutes before slicing.

MEATBALL, PEPPERONI AND CHEESE CALZONE/STROMBOLI

Who would have thought you could cook a calzone on the WSM? Here's a little snack we like to make when we're at barbecue contests. They are easy to make, and even easier to eat!

YIELD: 8 SERVINGS ★ COOK TIME: APPROXIMATELY 1 HOUR

---

1 pizza dough ball
8–12 slices provolone cheese
1 pound (455 g) pepperoni
8 meatballs (see page 107) or store-bought
1 jar pizza sauce

HD aluminum foil

Set up your WSM for high heat cooking (approximately 325–350°F [163–177°C]), and empty the water pan.

Roll out the pizza dough to a rectangle about 8 inches x 12 inches (20 centimeters x 30 centimeters). Lay out the cheese in the middle of the dough and add the slices of pepperoni. Next, you can add the meatballs and about a half jar of sauce, reserving the other half for dipping later on.

Fold in the left and right sides, and then fold in the front and back sides. Place the calzone seam side down onto the HD foil. Place it on the top rack of the WSM and cook for about 45–60 minutes or until the top becomes lightly browned.

Remove from the WSM and rest for about 15 minutes. Go ahead and slice it up, making sure that each piece has one whole meatball. Enjoy!

MOZZARELLA STUFFED MEATBALLS

These meatballs are fun to make. I love to watch people eat them for the first time, especially when they find a little surprise of melted cheese in the center of each one. These are great served with pasta, but keep them in mind for a meatball sandwich!

YIELD: 8 SERVINGS (1 MEATBALL EACH) ★ COOK TIME: APPROXIMATELY 1 HOUR

TOMATO SAUCE

1 garlic clove, minced
1 tsp (3 g) onion powder
1 tbsp (6 g) oregano
1 (28 ounce [795 g]) can tomato sauce
Salt and pepper to taste

2–3 slices white bread
¼ cup (60 ml) whole milk
1 pound (455 g) ground sirloin
1 pound (455 g) ground pork
1 garlic clove, minced
¼ cup (20 g) Parmesan cheese
Salt and pepper to taste
8 small fresh mozzarella balls
4 slices provolone cheese, cut in half

Set your WSM up for high heat cooking (approximately 300–350°F [149–177°C]).

To make the sauce, put all ingredients in a sauce pan and cook until heated through, about 15 minutes. Set aside.

Soak bread in milk until saturated, and then mix in ground sirloin, pork, garlic, Parmesan cheese, salt and pepper.

Make 8 patties and place a mozzarella ball in the center of each one and form into balls. Place meatballs directly on the cooking grate of the WSM, and cook at 300°F (149°C) for about 30 minutes. Put meatballs in pan, cover with sauce and cook for another 30 minutes covered. Remove cover and top with provolone cheese. Cover for 5–10 minutes so cheese melts.

LOADED POTATO WITH PULLED PORK

Here's a great recipe when you have some leftover pulled pork. Two great comfort foods mixed together: potato and pulled pork. What's not to love, right? The first time I had this was … you guessed it, at a barbecue contest. Do you see a familiar theme here yet? There was a festival going on, so we had some down time, and I took a walk around to check things out. We came across this small little booth just selling these potatoes. The line must have been 30 people deep! So, I thought, "Of course I'm waiting in line for this!" Man, was it worth it! Go ahead and give it a try.

YIELD: 4 SERVINGS ★ COOK TIME: APPROXIMATELY 1½ HOURS

4 large russet potatoes

Olive oil

Kosher salt

1 pound (455 g) leftover pulled pork (page 79), heated

4 tbsp (60 g) butter

1 cup (115 g) shredded cheddar cheese

½ pound (200 g) bacon, cooked and chopped

¼ cup (20 g) green onions

Sour cream

Fire up your WSM for hot and fast cooking (approximately 350–375°F [177–191°C]).

Wash and dry the potatoes, then rub them with olive oil and sprinkle them with kosher salt.

Place potatoes on the top rack of the WSM and cook for about 1½ hours, or until you can poke with a knife and feel no resistance.

Cut a lengthwise split in each potato and fluff the insides with a fork. Add the butter, pork, cheese and bacon and put back on the WSM for a few minutes to melt the cheese. Remove and serve with sour cream and green onions on top.

PIGS IN A BLANKET, GROWN UP STYLE

You probably haven't had these since you were a kid, right? Hot dogs and American cheese, rolled up in crescent rolls, and dipped in yellow mustard. Well, now that you're all grown up, you've probably moved on to bigger and better things. This recipe calls for a little ground pork, some sauerkraut and whole grain mustard—flavors that will satisfy. Go ahead and indulge. I'm bringing back a grown-up version of this all-time favorite, classic kid dish.

YIELD: 24 SERVINGS ★ COOK TIME: APPROXIMATELY 40 MINUTES

2 tbsp (30 g) unsalted butter

½ cup (120 g) minced shallot

4 large garlic cloves, minced

⅓ cup (40 g) panko bread crumbs

⅓ cup (80 ml) whole milk

1½ cups (215 g) drained sauerkraut

2 tbsp (30 g) whole grain or Dijon mustard, plus more for serving

1½ tsp (4 g) caraway seeds, toasted, lightly crushed

Kosher salt and freshly ground black pepper

1 pound (455 g) ground pork

2 (14 ounce [400 g]) packages frozen puff pastry, thawed

All-purpose flour (for dusting)

2 large eggs, beaten to blend

HD aluminum foil

Cooking spray

Set up the WSM for hot and fast cooking (approximately 325–380°F [163–193°C]).

Melt the butter in a small skillet over medium heat. Add shallot and cook until soft, 4–5 minutes. Add garlic and cook, about 1–2 minutes. Transfer mixture to a large bowl and let cool.

Combine panko and milk in a small bowl; let it stand until milk is absorbed, 2–3 minutes. Add panko and milk mixture to the bowl with the shallot mixture. Squeeze any excess liquid from the sauerkraut; coarsely chop and add it to the bowl. Stir in 1 tablespoon (15 grams) of Dijon mustard and caraway seeds; season with salt and pepper. Mix well. Add pork and gently mix until just combined.

Roll out puff pastry on a lightly floured surface to a 14 x 10-inch (36 x 25-centimeter) rectangle. Cut lengthwise into three 14 x 3-inch (36 x 8-centimeter) strips. Using one-third of the sausage filling leaving a 1-inch (2.5-centimeter) border at each end, form sausage into a thin log of filling down the center of 1 pastry strip. Fold pastry over sausage mixture to enclose and then press pastry together to seal. Fold seam under to ensure that the sausage is tightly wrapped. Repeat with remaining pastry and sausage mixture.

Cut small diagonal slits at 1-inch (2.5-centimeter) intervals along the top of the pastries (to help release steam). Brush the top and sides of the pastry with beaten egg; chill in the freezer for about 30 minutes.

Lay out a sheet of HD foil on the top grate of the WSM and spray with cooking spray. Place the grown pigs in a blanket on top of the foiled grate and cook for about 30–40 minutes or until pork is cooked through (about 145°F [63°C]). Remove from smoker and let rest for 5 minutes. Cut rolls into 1-inch (2.5-centimeter) pieces and serve with the extra mustard.

PIZZA-WRAPPED BURGER

You like pizza? You like burgers? Well look no further! It's the best of worlds: burgers and pizza served all together as one heaping pile of delicious.

YIELD: 4 SERVINGS ★ COOK TIME: APPROXIMATELY 30–45 MINUTES

1 pizza dough ball
1 pound (455 g) ground sirloin
1 pound (455 g) bacon, cooked
32 pepperoni slices
1 cup (7 g) roasted red peppers
1 cup (210 g) caramelized onions
8 slices cheddar cheese or 2 cups (230 g) shredded
Salt and pepper

Small round baking pan
Cooking spray

Set up the WSM for hot and fast cooking (approximately 325–380°F [163–193°C]).

Cut the ground sirloin into four equal portions; form into burger patties and season with salt and pepper.

Roll out pizza dough to about 12 inches (30 centimeters) and cut into 4 pieces—from there you can roll out each piece a little more.

Now time to build the burger, but you are going to be building it upside down. You'll see why later.

Lay out the pizza dough, and add the cheese, bacon, pepperoni, onions, peppers, the burger and more cheese. Now, start to bring the corners together (you will want to take a little bit of water and wet the edges of the dough to help it bond together).

Flip the burger over and place it onto a small round (12–16 inch [30–40 centimeter]) baking pan sprayed with non stick cooking spray so that the seam is facing down.

Cook in the WSM for 30–45 minutes, until the internal temperature of the burger is approximately 135–140°F (57–60°C). Remove and let it rest for about 10 minutes.

You can serve this with any condiment you want, chipotle mayo, ketchup and mustard or even pizza sauce! Enjoy.

PORK BELLY SLIDERS, ASIAN STYLE

The Asian slaw is the perfect complement to the richness of the pork belly and brings along with it the chipotle mayo. Oh, man—what a perfect combination! Yeah, it's that good!!!

YIELD: 12 SERVINGS ★ COOK TIME: 2½ HOURS

PORK
2–3 pounds (1–1.5 kg) cured/smoked pork belly (see page 77)
1 (12 ounce [340 ml]) bottle of dark beer
Salt and pepper

ASIAN SLAW
2 carrots, peeled and julienned
½ English cucumber, seeded and julienned
½ Fuji apple, julienned
½ red onion, thinly sliced
¼ cup (4 g) cilantro
¼ cup (60 ml) rice wine vinegar
¼ cup (60 ml) mirin
1 tsp (4 g) sugar
2 tbsp (5 g) light soy sauce
Pinch or more of red pepper flakes, to taste

CHIPOTLE MAYONNAISE
⅓ cup (80 g) mayonnaise
1 medium canned chipotle pepper in adobo sauce, finely chopped
1 tsp (6 g) adobo sauce

1 dozen slider buns
Arugula

To make the pork, set up your WSM for high heat cooking (approximately 300–350°F [149–177°C]).

Score the fat cap in crisscross sections through the fat, but not into the meat itself. Generously coat with salt and pepper, rubbing into the crisscross sections and on all sides of the meat.

Place in a roasting pan with beer, fat side up and cook in the WSM for 2 hours. After 2 hours, remove the roasting pan and cook over direct heat to crisp up the top, basting every 10 minutes until crunchy on top.

Remove from the WSM and let it cool. You can make this ahead of time and put it in the refrigerator until you're ready to make sandwiches.

To make the slaw, combine all of the ingredients in a bowl. Put it in the refrigerator to chill for an hour or longer so the flavors blend.

To make the mayo, combine all of the ingredients in a bowl. Chill it in the refrigerator until you're ready to assemble the sandwiches.

When you're ready to assemble the sandwich, slice the pork belly into ¼-inch (6-millimeter) slices. If pork has been reserved in the refrigerator, reheat slices in a frying pan. Slice the slider buns in half, and slather the sides with chipotle mayonnaise. Then layer arugula, two pork belly slices and a heaping of Asian slaw mixture. Top with bun and serve.

SMOKED LOBSTER TAIL

One of the things New Englanders are known for is lobster. It's pretty much the main staple at any clambake during summer. These smoked lobster tails might be one of the easiest dishes you'll ever make in your smoker. I'm guessing they'll be one of the tastiest, too.

YIELD: 6 SERVINGS ★ COOK TIME: APPROXIMATELY 20–30 MINUTES

6 lobster tails
½ cup (115 g) unsalted butter
6 cloves garlic, chopped
Salt and pepper to taste

1 chunk of apple wood

Set up your WSM for high heat cooking (approximately 350°F [177°C]), using an empty water pan.

With the shell facing up, open the lobster tails with poultry or heavy duty kitchen scissors. Release the lobster meat from inside of the shell by running your finger on the inside of the shell between the meat and shell. Season with salt and pepper.

Melt butter with garlic over medium-low heat. Drizzle this over the lobster meat on the inside of opened shell, between the lobster meat and shell, making sure to get some garlic in there.

Place onto the top rack of your smoker (shell down) and cook until the internal temperature registers at 130–145°F (55–63°C). Remove from the heat and allow it to rest for a few minutes. Then, slide a fork underneath the lobster meat and lift it out and onto the top of the lobster tail shell.

Serve with additional garlic butter.

WEST COAST-STYLE TRI-TIP

Here in the Northeast, it seems that not a lot people have heard about tri-tip. It's very popular out on the West Coast. Tri-tip is a triangular cut of meat found at the bottom of the sirloin. It's well marbled, tender and one of the most flavorful cuts of beef you'll find. Most of the tri-tip you'll find at the supermarket weighs around 2–2½ pounds (910–1,200 grams). It's the perfect cut of meat for cooking hot and fast. In this recipe, I'm using my interpretation of a classic West Coast–style rub: a little salt and pepper, mixed with fresh herbs and a touch of heat to really bring out the flavor of the meat. "Tri" some, you're going to love it.

YIELD: ABOUT 4–6 SERVINGS ★ COOK TIME: APPROXIMATELY 20–40 MINUTES

RUB

1 tbsp (15 g) kosher salt
1 tbsp (7 g) coarse ground black pepper
1 tbsp (10 g) garlic powder
1 tbsp (7 g) onion powder
1 tsp (2 g) cayenne
1 tbsp (3 g) fresh oregano, chopped finely
1 tsp (5 g) fresh rosemary, finely minced
½ tsp fresh sage, chopped finely

2 tri-tip roasts (about 2 pounds [910 g] each)
Olive oil

2 chunks of oak wood
HD aluminum foil

Fire up the WSM for high heat cooking (approximately 350°F [177°C]). For this recipe, leave out the water pan, and wrap the bottom grate with HD foil. Add the wood chunks about 5 minutes before cooking.

Mix the dry rub ingredients together completely and set it aside until ready to use.

Lightly coat the tri-tip roasts with olive oil and apply the rub to both sides of the tri-tip and let it sit out for about an hour. Place onto the bottom rack of the WSM for 5 minutes, then flip and cook for another 5 minutes. Remove and place on the top rack and continue cooking until desired doneness, 120–125°F (49–52°C) for rare, 130–135°F (55–57°C) medium rare—this could take 20–40 minutes depending on the thickness and size of the tri-tip.

Remove from the WSM and rest loosely tented for about 10 minutes. Slice against the grain and serve.

➻ For high heat, indirect cooking, you can wrap the bottom grate in aluminum foil so that it acts as a heat sink. This is just a handy alternative that provides the same effect as wrapping an empty water pan.

NOT YOUR AVERAGE CHICKEN CORDON BLEU

In a typical chicken cordon bleu recipe, ham and Swiss cheese are rolled up inside a chicken breast and fried until crispy. In this version, we use salty prosciutto and nutty Gruyère cheese, and for some for extra flavor, we coat the chicken with Dijon mustard and panko bread crumbs.

YIELD: 4 SERVINGS ★ COOK TIME: APPROXIMATELY 30–45 MINUTES

4 chicken breasts
Salt and pepper
8 slices prosciutto
1 cup (110 g) Gruyère cheese, shredded
½ cup (125 g) Dijon mustard
2 cups (240 g) panko bread crumbs

16 toothpicks
2 chunks of apple wood

Fire up your WSM for high heat cooking (about 350°F [177°C]), using an empty foiled water pan. Add the smoke wood about 5 minutes before putting the chicken on.

Loosely wrap each chicken breast in plastic. Take a meat mallet and pound each breast until even thickness about ½ inch (13 millimeters) thick, then season with salt and pepper. Lay out 2 slices of prosciutto on top of the chicken in a cross pattern, and add about ¼ cup (30 grams) of Gruyère cheese. Wrap the cheese up with the prosciutto into a package and place onto the center of the flattened chicken breast. Roll the chicken up and secure with toothpicks. Coat the outside of the chicken with mustard and roll it in the panko bread crumbs.

Place on the top grate of the WSM, and cook until you get an internal temperature of 165°F (74°C). Remove from cooker and let it sit for 5 minutes, then serve.

CHICKEN BOMBS

These tasty little chicken treats are perfect for your next cookout, the little bit of heat from the jalapeño and the sweetness of the BBQ sauce are a match made in heaven. The only bad thing is your friends are going to be asking you to cook them for all your parties!

YIELD: 10 SERVINGS ★ COOK TIME: APPROXIMATELY 45 MINUTES

5 boneless skinless chicken breasts
Salt and pepper
Smokin' Hoggz All-Purpose Rub (page 35)
8 ounces (230 g) cream cheese, softened
1 cup (115 g) Colby-Monterey Jack cheese
10 slices cheddar cheese
5 jalapeños, sliced in half lengthwise and cleaned
20 slices bacon
1 cup (240 g) BBQ Sauce (page 23)

Heat up your WSM for high heat cooking (approximately 350°F [177°C]).

Slice chicken breasts in half (like a hamburger bun). Place them in a plastic gallon-sized bag and pound until ¼ inch (6 millimeters) thick. Season with salt and pepper and the all-purpose rub.

Mix the cream cheese and Colby/Jack together and smear about 2 tablespoons (15 grams) into each pepper half (use up the cheese between all of the peppers). Take the cheddar cheese slices and wrap around pepper.

Place the pepper on the chicken breast and wrap it up as best you can. I suggest placing the pepper cheese-side down so it gets completely covered by the chicken. Season the outside of the chicken lightly with some rub. Wrap each chicken breast completely with two to three pieces of bacon. Start at one end, wrap half the breast and finish the second half with the other piece of bacon. Apply more rub to the outside of the bacon.

Place onto the WSM and cook for 30–45 minutes or until chicken is done (165°F [74°C]). Towards the last 15 minutes, apply a thin layer of BBQ sauce.

Remove from the WSM and let it rest for about 5–10 minutes, slice in half, then serve.

(continued)

CHICKEN BOMBS (CONTINUED)

➤ Applying rub to chicken

➤ A little more rub

➤ Brushing chicken with sauce

➤ Slicing in half

PORK OSSO BUCCO

Osso Bucco is a traditional Italian dish using veal shanks. Veal shanks can be expensive and sometimes they're hard to find. I like to use pork shanks because they are less expensive and a lot easier to find. I think the dish comes out just as good with pork as it does with the veal. Osso Bucco may seem hard to make, but it's actually pretty easy, and very tasty. It's smoked for about an hour, then braised in a Dutch oven for a couple hours for a melt-in-your-mouth finish.

YIELD: 4 SERVINGS ★ COOK TIME: APPROXIMATELY 3–4 HOURS

4–6 meaty slices of pork shank, cut 1½" (4 cm) thick

Olive oil

Ground black pepper to taste

Salt to taste

⅓ cup (45 g) carrots, diced

⅓ cup (55 g) onions, diced

⅓ cup (35 g) celery, diced

4 cloves garlic, minced

1 cup (240 ml) dry white wine

1 cup (240 ml) chicken stock

GREMOLATA

1 tbsp (6 g) lemon zest, minced

¼ cup (15 g) fresh parsley, finely chopped

3 cloves garlic, finely chopped

Cast iron Dutch oven with lid

2 chunks apple wood

Prepare your WSM for the lower end of high heat cooking, about 325°F (163°C). Use an empty foil-lined water pan (easy clean up). Add your smoke wood a few minutes before putting the meat on. Also, put the Dutch oven on the bottom grate, this is to heat it up so it will be ready for braising the shanks during the second part of the cook.

Drizzle olive oil over each pork shank and rub it in. Season with salt and pepper.

Add the carrots, onions, celery, garlic, white wine and chicken stock to the Dutch oven (cover off). At the same time place the pork shanks on the top grate of the WSM and cook for one hour.

Place the pork shanks into Dutch oven (bottom grate) and cover; cook until pork is fork tender, about 2–3 hours.

Mix ingredients for the Gremolata; set aside until ready to use.

Remove the pork shank from Dutch oven and reduce liquid by half over medium heat, about 15 minutes. Add Gremolata, return shanks to pan and spoon sauce over shank. Serve and enjoy!

MEATLOAF

If you've never had smoked meatloaf, then you've been missing out on one of barbecue's best dishes! Here's a recipe that's going to make you want to eat the pan you cook it on, never mind the actual meatloaf itself. The smoke flavor and the sweetness of the glaze really make this dish come together.

YIELD: ABOUT 8–10 SERVINGS ★ COOK TIME: APPROXIMATELY 2½ HOURS

MEATLOAF
1 pound (455 g) ground sirloin
1 pound (455 g) ground veal
1 pound (455 g) ground pork
2 eggs
¼ cup (40 g) chopped onion
3 cloves garlic minced
½ cup (120 g) ketchup
¼ cup (60 ml) milk
⅔ cup (50 g) crackers crushed into crumbs
1 tbsp (15 g) kosher salt
½ tsp black pepper

MEATLOAF SAUCE
½ cup (120 g) ketchup
¼ cup (50 g) brown sugar (light or dark)
1 tbsp (6 g) chili powder
1 tsp (5 g) kosher salt

12" (30 cm) round disposable pan
with holes in it
Cooking spray
HD aluminum foil
3 small chunks of wood

Mix all of the meatloaf ingredients together and place onto the pan and form into a log.

Mix the meatloaf sauce ingredients together and store in a bowl in the fridge.

Set up the WSM for hot and fast cooking. This means running the cooker at about 350°F (177°C) with an empty, foil-lined water pan for easy cleanup.

Fire-up a chimney full of charcoal briquettes and dump the hot coals into the charcoal chamber; dump another ¾ chimney of unlit briquettes over the lit coals. When all the coals are hot, assemble the cooker and put the meatloaf on the top grate.

Now you can add about 3 small chunks of wood—oak, pecan or apple would be good choices—but don't use too much or you run the risk of over-smoking, which will give you a bitter taste. Open the top vent and all three bottom vents fully. Once the cooker comes up to temperature, adjust the bottom vents to maintain 350°F (177°C) for the entire cooking session.

Place the meatloaf on the top rack of the WSM, and cook for about an hour; apply about half the sauce, reserving the rest for dipping later. Cook for another 1–1½ hours or until it reaches an internal temperature of 160°F (72°C). Remove from the WSM, tent with foil and rest for about 15 minutes. Slice and enjoy with some mashed potatoes.

RACK OF LAMB

Most of the lamb we buy in grocery stores comes from New Zealand, and the tops of the bones are already trimmed (or "Frenched"). If you have a butcher near you and can get your hands on some domestic lamb, you want to do so because the flavor is fantastic! If you get the lamb from a butcher, chances are the tops of the bones won't be trimmed. If you are feeling brave and ambitious enough, you can try to French (trim) the bones yourself. However, if you are like me, you'll let the professional butchers do it. Chances are they can do it far more quickly than I can, and they'll keep all their fingers intact.

YIELD: 4 SERVINGS ★ COOK TIME: APPROXIMATELY 1 HOUR

1 bone rack of lamb, trimmed and Frenched (all the fat is trimmed from the bone, makes like a handle)

PASTE
4 cloves of garlic, finely minced
2 tbsp (4 g) fresh rosemary, minced
1 tbsp (30 ml) olive oil
1 tbsp (30 ml) white wine
½ stick softened butter
2 tsp (10 g) kosher salt
2 tsp (5 g) black pepper
½ tsp onion powder
½ tsp dried thyme
½ tsp coriander
½ tsp crushed red pepper flakes

2–3 black cherry wood chunks
HD aluminum foil (optional)

Set up your cooker for high heat cooking, about 350°F (163°C), with an empty foiled water pan (for easy clean up). Add your smoke wood about 5 minutes before putting the lamb on the cooker.

Mix ingredients in a bowl to make into a paste. Rub the paste evenly over the rack of lamb. Cover with plastic wrap and let sit in the fridge for 3 hours before cooking.

If you want, you can wrap the top of the bones with foil, this will help prevent the bones from burning. If you're not trying to impress anyone and don't mind the bones getting a little dark in color, just leave them be.

Lightly oil the top grate and place the rack of lamb in the center bone-side down to help create crust on the surface of the meat. Cook until the internal temperature is about 145°F (63°C), about 1 hour.

Remove from the cooker and allow a rest time of about 10 minutes before cutting it up and serving.

HAM

One of the things I love about the holiday season is that someone in my family will be cooking ham. It's just not the holidays without it! I love that savory salty flavor mixed in with the sweetness of the glaze! I like to use a "ready to cook" ham, which means the ham has already been cured and partially cooked, and all you have to do is finish cooking it to 155–160°F (68–71°C). It's easy, plus you can still add your favorite seasoning and add a little bit of smoke flavor.

YIELD: ABOUT 16 SERVINGS ★ COOK TIME: APPROXIMATELY 2-3 HOURS

1 ready-to-cook ham (16 pounds [7.25 kg])
Smokin' Hoggz All-Purpose Rub (page 35)
Ham Glaze (page 129)

HD aluminum foil
3–4 chunks apple wood

Set up your WSM for high heat cooking (approximately 325°F [163°C]), use an empty water pan lined with foil, for easy clean up. Add your smoke wood at the same time you put the ham on.

When you take the ham out of its packaging, it'll probably have a thin jelly-like layer on it, so you just want to run it under cold water and rinse it off, then pat dry with a paper towel.

Next, score the fat with the traditional diamond/checkerboard pattern you normally see with hams—not only does it look great after it's cooked, it also helps with rendering the fat during the cooking process. To do this, take your knife and cut ¼-inch (6-millimeter) deep lines about 1 inch (2.5 centimeters) apart, then again perpendicular to the cuts you just made.

Season lightly all over with rub. Let your ham sit out on the counter for about 1–2 hours.

Put your ham on the top rack of cooker and cook until you get an internal temperature of about 155°F (68°C). This is probably going to take about 3 hours, so start checking the temperature at the 2-hour mark. You can also start applying the glaze at this point too.

When the ham reaches temperature, remove it and let it rest for about 30 minutes, loosely tented with aluminum foil. Slice and serve.

HAM GLAZE

What's a holiday ham without a glaze? I'm not talking about the little packet that comes with an already cooked ham. No, I'm talking about making your own. You're going to love this glaze! You will notice there is no salt in this recipe. It really doesn't need any because of all the salt in the ham. What I like about this glaze is the sweetness of the honey, the background savory flavor the mustard brings and the subtle hint of heat from the chipotles. It all makes this a perfect glaze for your holiday ham.

YIELD: ABOUT 2 CUPS (640 G) ★ COOK TIME: APPROXIMATELY 15 MINUTES

1 cup (240 ml) cider vinegar
½ pound (230 g) dark brown sugar
½ cup (170 g) honey
¼ cup (60 ml) pineapple juice
2 tbsp (30 g) Dijon mustard
¼ tsp chipotle powder

In a medium-sized saucepan, heat up the vinegar and add the brown sugar, stirring until the sugar is dissolved. Remove from heat, add the remaining ingredients and mix well. Return to medium/low heat and simmer about 15–20 minutes.

APPLE STREUSEL CHEESECAKE BARS

Apple, oatmeal and cheesecake, that's all that needs to be said for this. I will be surprised if you don't eat the whole tray in one sitting!!!

YIELD: 20 SERVINGS ★ COOK TIME: APPROXIMATELY 40 MINUTES

1 pouch (1 pound 1½ ounces [500 g]) oatmeal cookie mix

½ cup (115 g) firm butter or margarine

2 packages (8 ounces [230 g] each) cream cheese, softened

½ cup (95 g) sugar

2 tbsp (15 g) all-purpose flour

1 tsp (5 ml) vanilla

1 egg

1 (21 ounce [600 g]) can apple pie filling

½ tsp ground cinnamon

¼ cup (30 g) chopped walnuts

Fire up the WSM for high heat cooking to 350°F (177°C). Spray bottom and sides of 13 x 9-inch (33 x 23-centimeter) pan with cooking spray. Place cookie mix in large bowl. With a fork, cut in the butter until the mixture is crumbly and coarse. Reserve 1½ cups (180 grams) crumb mixture; press remaining crumbs in bottom of the pan. Bake for 10 minutes.

Meanwhile, in a large bowl, beat cream cheese, sugar, flour, vanilla and egg with an electric mixer on medium speed until smooth. Spread the cream cheese mixture evenly over the partially baked crust. In a medium bowl, mix the pie filling and cinnamon. Spoon this evenly over the cream cheese mixture. Sprinkle reserved crumbs over the top. Sprinkle with walnuts.

Cook for 35–40 minutes longer or until it is a light golden brown. Cool for about 30 minutes. Refrigerate to chill, about 2 hours. For the bars, cut into 6 rows by 4 rows. Store covered in the refrigerator.

MINI WHITE CHOCOLATE RASPBERRY CHEESECAKE

Cheesecake is probably one of the most decadent desserts around. There are so many different flavors to choose from: chocolate, strawberry, cherry, pumpkin, red velvet, snickers bar, tiramisu … the list goes on and on. This is one of my wife's favorite dessert recipes and it's won multiple awards at several contests. It's light and refreshing, and since they are mini cheesecakes, you don't have the guilt most of us suffer after eating a luxurious dessert.

Note: I use a mini cheesecake pan for this recipe. The bottom of each well has a removable disk that can be pushed up through the hole in the bottom, making it easy to remove the cheesecake from the pan. If you don't have a mini cheesecake pan, you can also use a cupcake pan with cupcake liners.

YIELD: 12 SERVINGS ★ COOK TIME: APPROXIMATELY 18 MINUTES

CRUST
¼ cup (25 g) fine chocolate cookie crumbs
2 tbsp (30 ml) butter, melted

FILLING
1–1½ packages cream cheese (8 ounces [23 g] each), softened
⅓ cup (65 g) sugar
2 eggs
1 tsp (5 ml) vanilla
2 ounces (60 g) white chocolate, melted
½ pint (130 g) raspberries

Set up you cooker for high heat cooking (approximately 350°F [177°C]), using lump charcoal and an empty water pan.

To make the crust, pulse cookies in a food processor until fine. Add the melted butter and pulse to combine. If you do not have a food processor, you can put the cookies in a zippered plastic bag and roll them with a rolling pin until the cookies are crushed and fine. Place 1 heaping tablespoon (7 grams) of cookie crumbs in each mini cheesecake pan and press down with a small spoon. Refrigerate until ready to use.

To make the filling, beat cream cheese until smooth and gradually add sugar until smooth. Add the eggs, vanilla and melted chocolate. Spoon a small amount of cream cheese mixture into each tin. Slice raspberries in half and lay flat on this layer. Fill in with the remaining mixture to top.

Place on the top grate of the WSM, and cook for 15–18 minutes or until set. You will know cheesecake is done when you can lightly tap the top and it is firm. Also, you can jiggle the pan a little—if the mini cheesecakes don't jiggle in the center, they're done.

Let them cool on a rack for 20 minutes and remove from tin. Let them cool completely on a tray. Refrigerate for at least an hour before serving. When serving you can garnish with some caramel sauce and top with a raspberry.

INDIVIDUAL PEACH COBBLER

Peach cobbler is a great summer treat to have at any BBQ. Cooking the peaches on the smoker brings out the great flavor of the peach and adds a sweet caramelization. My wife created this dessert and it's the first dessert dish we ever placed in. It won second place dessert at the New England BBQ Championship held at the Harpoon Brewery in Windsor, Vermont.

YIELD: 12 SERVINGS ★ COOK TIME: APPROXIMATELY 45 MINUTES

CRUST
1 package Pillsbury Pie Dough

FILLING
6–8 peaches, cut in half and pitted
Olive oil
½ cup (115 g) unsalted butter
¼ cup (50 g) brown sugar
¼ tsp cinnamon
⅛ tsp ground nutmeg
1 tsp (5 ml) lemon juice
2 tsp (5 g) cornstarch
Granola cereal, garnish
Caramel sauce, garnish

Muffin pan with 12 spots

Set up your WSM for high heat cooking (approximately 350°F [177°C]). For the first part of this recipe, you will be cooking on the top grate using an empty water pan. For the second part, you're cooking on the bottom grate without the water pan. You finish on the top grate with an empty water pan.

To make the crust, unroll the package of dough. Using a round cookie cutter, slightly larger than the muffin tin, cut out circles. Press the circles into the non-stick muffin pan. Place the pan on the top rack of smoker (with an empty water pan) and cook until dough is a golden brown. Cool dough and remove from muffin tin.

To make the filling, lightly brush cut-side of peaches with olive oil (remove the water pan) and place them on grate cut-side down. Cook for about 5 minutes or until flesh is caramelized. Cut the peaches into small chunks.

In a half pan, combine peaches, brown sugar, cinnamon, nutmeg, lemon juice, butter and cornstarch. Place back on the grate of smoker and cook for 15 minutes or until filling has a thick consistency.

To assemble, fill each dough cup with peach filling. Sprinkle with granola and caramel sauce.

➵ **When you remove the water pan and cook the peaches on the bottom grate, it will help sugars on the flesh side of the peaches caramelize, creating layers of flavor.**

CAST IRON APPLE CRISP

Who doesn't like Apple Crisp? It's a great fall dessert. I can remember growing up and my grandmother would always have either an apple pie or an apple crisp for the holidays. I love the scent of apples and cinnamon cooking. Here's our little twist on this fall classic.

YIELD: 8 SERVINGS ★ COOK TIME: APPROXIMATELY 55 MINUTES

6 Cortland apples (peeled, cored and sliced)
¾ cup (150 g) packed brown sugar
½ cup (50 g) all-purpose flour
½ cup (40 g) rolled oats
¾ tsp cinnamon
¾ tsp nutmeg
⅓ cup (80 g) butter, softened

9" (23 cm) large cast iron skillet

Preheat smoker to 350°F (177°C). Put sliced apples into the large 9-inch (23-centimeter) cast iron skillet. In a bowl, combine the oats, flour, sugar, nutmeg, cinnamon and butter. Mix until well combined. Spread the topping in an even layer over the apples and bake for 45–55 minutes, or until the topping is crisp and brown and the apples are cooked through. You may have to cook a bit longer, just watch closely.

PINEAPPLE UPSIDE-DOWN CAKE

Pineapple upside-down cake is one of those cakes that is easy to make, and once finished, looks so yummy with its caramelized pineapples. It's one of those dishes that is great to bring to any potluck or summer picnic.

YIELD: 12 SERVINGS ★ COOK TIME: APPROXIMATELY 45 MINUTES

1 (18.25 ounce [520 g]) package Duncan Hines Moist Deluxe Pineapple Supreme Cake Mix

½ cup (115 g) butter

1 cup (200 g) firmly packed brown sugar

1 (20 ounce [570 g]) can pineapple slices, drained

¼ cup (25 g) red maraschino cherries

1 cast iron skillet

Preheat the WSM to 350°F (177°C) (hot and fast cooking).

Melt butter in a cast iron skillet. Sprinkle brown sugar evenly in skillet. Arrange pineapple slices evenly on the brown sugar. Place maraschino cherry halves in the center of the pineapple slices.

Prepare the cake mix following package directions for basic recipe. Pour batter evenly over fruit in the skillet. Bake at 350°F (177°C) for 45 minutes or until a toothpick inserted in center comes out clean. Cool for 5 minutes in the pan. Flip it onto a cake plate and serve.

CHAPTER THREE

THE SECRETS TO COMBINATION COOKING ON THE ⟨WSM⟩ AND OTHER SMOKERS

Combination cooking uses both high heat and low and slow cooking techniques. This chapter contains a variety of fun and delicious recipes that either start using the low and slow technique and finish with a blast of high heat, or start with the fast cooking techniques then end with a slow cook.

BASIC WORKFLOW FOR LOW AND SLOW TO HOT AND FAST:

1. Dump one chimney of unlit charcoal in the charcoal ring. We recommend using natural briquettes because they're better suited for the low and slow style of cooking.

2. Add about 10–15 lit briquettes to the pile of unlit charcoal. This will bring the WSM to a temperature of approximately 250°F (121°C).

3. Fill the water pan about one-half to three-quarters with hot water. Cook for however long the recipe says, keeping the top vent fully open.

4. Make sure the bottom vents are fully open. When the WSM gets within 50°F (10°C) of the cooking temperature the recipe specifies, close the bottom vents halfway and continue to monitor the temperature.

5. When the WSM attains the cooking temperature specified in the recipe, place the meat on the cooking grates. Let the food cook for the length of time specified in the recipe. As the last 15 minutes of cook time approach, start a full batch of charcoal using a charcoal chimney. We recommend using lump charcoal, as it is better suited for the hot and fast style of cooking

6. Continue to follow the instructions in the recipe you are using. At some point, you will be told to temporarily remove the food from the WSM so you can change over to the hot and fast cooking method.

7. Carefully remove the center section of the WSM, and empty the water pan.

8. Depending on the recipe you are using, you will either place an empty water pan in position or use no water pan at all.

9. Carefully dump the hot charcoal from the charcoal chimney into the charcoal ring.

10. Reassemble the WSM, open all vents and wait for the temperature to stabilize at approximately 350°F (177°C).

11. If you are having trouble maintaining the high temperature, prop open the side access door about ½ inch (13 millimeters); the added air flow will help raise the temperature.

BASIC WORKFLOW FOR HOT AND FAST TO LOW AND SLOW:

1. Carefully pour one full chimney of lit charcoal into the charcoal ring. We recommend using lump charcoal because it burns hotter than briquettes and is better suited for the hot and fast style of cooking.

2. Make sure all of the vents are fully open.

3. Depending on the recipe, you will either use an empty water pan covered in foil, and cook on the top grate, or you will remove the water pan and cook on the bottom grate. Either way, you want to attain a temperature of 350–400°F (177–205°C).

4. Continue to follow the instructions for the recipe you are using. At some point, you will be told to temporarily remove the food from the WSM so you can change over to the low and slow cooking method.

5. Remove middle section of the WSM, and add about one-and-a-half chimneys of unlit charcoal to the ring.

6. Reassemble the WSM and add cool water to the water pan. Adding cool water will help bring the temperature down.

7. Close the bottom vents all the way, depleting the hot charcoals of oxygen, and closely monitor the temperature of the WSM.

8. When the temperature reaches approximately 250°F (121°C) (or whatever "low" temperature the recipe specifies), open the bottom vents a quarter to halfway, to help maintain the temperature.

9. If you are having trouble bringing the temperature down, add cold water to the water pan, and then completely close all the vents.

CHICKEN WINGS

Who doesn't love chicken wings, right? Wings are one of the greatest bar foods of all time, and there are many different flavors to choose from. Not only am I going to show you how to cook wings so they have crispy skin and moist meat, I'm also sharing some of my favorite wing sauces!

First, you want to set up your WSM for low and slow cooking. Take one chimney of unlit lump charcoal and dump it into the center of the charcoal ring. Make a small nest in the unlit charcoal so you can add the lit charcoal when it's ready. Next you'll want to fill your chimney about halfway and light it. It should only take about 10 minutes for it to be ready to dump on the unlit charcoal.

Assemble the WSM and fill the water pan with warm water. Keep all three vents fully open until you are about 50°F (10°C) from your desired cooking temp (250°F [121°C]). From there, close the bottom vents halfway. Once the desired cooking temperature is reached, you'll probably be able to keep the vents about 25 percent open.

Now here's a tip so that you don't lose temperature while you're putting the wings on the WSM. Keep the cooking grates out of the cooker while it's heating up. Place the wings on the grates and when the WSM is up to temperature, lift off the cover and place the grates with the wings into the WSM. It should only take about 20–30 seconds, and you won't lose much of that heat that built up inside the cooker. At this point, open the side door and place a couple of chunks of fruitwood directly onto the coals. Around my neck of the woods, apple and sugar maple are pretty common, so that's what I use. But you can use any kind of hardwood you like.

Let the wings cook for about 1½ hours. Keep checking the temperature and open and close your vents accordingly.

At about 1 hour and 15 minutes into the cook, go ahead and light a full charcoal chimney. At 1½ hours into the cook, remove the entire center section of the WSM (keeping the cover on), and dump the lit chimney into the charcoal ring. Let it sit for 5 minutes—during that time, remove the water pan from the WSM. Place the middle section back onto the base and cook for 10 more minutes. Flip the wings and cook for an additional 10 minutes. This will help to crisp them up.

Place the wings into a bowl and toss with sauce.

➵ **Note: All of these wing recipes call for 5 pounds (2.25 kilograms) of wings (whole or wings and drummettes) and will serve about 6–8 people. Cook time is approximately 2 hours.**

(continued)

→ Putting the wings on the WSM

→ Adding the sauce

BUFFALO WINGS

I love Buffalo wings, and I order them every time I go out to watch football or any game for that matter. This recipe will get your friends talking—and by talking, I mean asking you to make these wings for the next big game.

SAUCE

¼ stick butter
1 cup (240 ml) hot sauce
2 tbsp (30 ml) Sriracha sauce
¼ cup (60 ml) Italian dressing
¼ cup (60 ml) agave
1 tbsp (8 g) chili powder
Salt and pepper

RUB

Season the wings with some salt and pepper and a little dusting of chili powder. Let them sit in the fridge for about an hour then remove just before they go on the WSM.

While the wings are cooking, you can go ahead and make the wing sauce. In a saucepan, melt the butter on medium heat then stir in the rest of the ingredients. Simmer for 5 minutes, and add the salt and pepper to taste. When the wings come off the WSM, throw them in a big bowl and toss with the buffalo wing sauce.

SWEET THAI CHILI WINGS

This sauce is so much better than the stuff you get in stores. It's versatile, and you can use it on a lot of different things, such as grilled or fried shrimp, egg rolls or even as base for pizza. But my favorite—my favorite is using it on wings!

RUB
Season the wings with salt and pepper and some crushed red pepper flakes.

SAUCE
3 cloves garlic
2 red jalapeños or serrano peppers, very finely diced
¼ cup (60 ml) rice wine vinegar
½ cup (120 ml) agave
¾ cup (180 ml) water
1 tsp (5 ml) ketchup
1 tsp (5 ml) Sriracha
½ tsp salt
1 tbsp (10 g) cornstarch
2 tbsp (30 ml) water

In the blender, mix together all the ingredients, except for the last two. Transfer the mixture to a saucepan and bring to a boil over medium-high heat. Lower the heat to medium and simmer until the mixture thickens up a bit and the garlic-pepper bits begin to soften, about 3 minutes. Combine the cornstarch and water to make a slurry. Whisk in the cornstarch mixture and continue to simmer 1 more minute. The cornstarch will help the sauce to thicken slightly, thereby causing nice suspension of the garlic-pepper bits; otherwise, you get a thin sauce with all the little pieces floating on the surface. Let cool completely before storing in a glass jar and refrigerate.

TERIYAKI

Teriyaki wings are some of my favorite wings. They seem to be a staple at birthday parties and at every summer cookout. These wings will be a big hit at any event you go to.

RUB
2 tbsp (30 g) salt
1 tsp (3 g) coarse black pepper
2 tbsp (25 g) white sugar
1 tsp (2 g) onion powder
2 tsp (6 g) chili powder
1 tbsp (10 g) garlic
1 tsp (2 g) ginger powder
1 tsp (2 g) mustard powder

SAUCE
½ cup (120 ml) soy sauce
2 tbsp (30 ml) mirin (sweet cooking rice wine)
2 tbsp (30 ml) rice wine vinegar
1 tbsp (15 ml) sesame oil
½ cup (100 g) brown sugar
2 tbsp (15 g) grated ginger
4 cloves garlic
2 scallions, diced
½ tsp black pepper

Mix all of the ingredients together, and store in an airtight container until ready to use. Season the wings with the rub and let sit for about 30 minutes before putting them on the WSM.

In a saucepan, combine all of the ingredients and simmer until the sugar is fully dissolved. When the wings are done, place them into a large bowl and toss with the sauce.

DRY-SEASONED WINGS

You know sometimes you just want a well-seasoned wing. This recipe provides just that—a well-seasoned wing, cooked perfectly and that tastes awesome! Sometimes, it's the simple things that bring the most pleasure. Now, have at it!

¼ cup (60 g) kosher salt
2 tbsp (25 g) sugar
2 tbsp (25 g) brown sugar
1 tsp (3 g) garlic powder
1 tsp (2 g) onion powder
2 tsp (5 g) paprika
2 tsp (5 g) chili powder

Mix all of the ingredients in a bowl and store in an airtight container until ready to use.

After the wings come off the WSM, toss liberally with wing seasoning.

WHITE BBQ SAUCE

This traditional Alabama barbecue sauce uses mayonnaise as its base, rather than tomato sauce, vinegar or any of the other traditional barbecue sauce bases. Like many barbecue sauces, you want to apply this only at the very end of your grilling or smoking. White sauce will break down and separate if it is heated too long. Use this sauce on chicken and turkey. It is also good on pork. Alabama white barbecue sauce has a tangy flavor that is a great addition to grilled or smoked foods. The first time I ever had this sauce was at my friend's wood-fired pizza restaurant. He told me, "You have to try it; it will blow your mind!" Here is my rendition of this Alabama classic.

COOK TIME: APPROXIMATELY 3–4 HOURS

RUB
Season the wings lightly with salt and pepper.

SAUCE
2 cups (450 g) mayonnaise
1 cup (240 ml) cider vinegar
¼ cup (60 ml) agave
1 tsp (3 g) garlic powder
2 tsp (5 g) chili powder
1 tbsp (7 g) coarse black pepper
1 tbsp (15 g) salt

Mix all of the ingredients in a bowl and store in the fridge. When wings come off the WSM, place them in a bowl and toss with some of the white BBQ sauce.

PORCHETTA

In my opinion, porchetta is one of the greatest dishes ever created. Basically, porchetta is an old Italian tradition of stuffing a piece of pork inside another piece of pork, and cooking it until perfection. It's usually sliced thin and served in either a sandwich or just by itself. Either way, you won't be disappointed with this porkie goodness.

YIELD: 20 SERVINGS ★ COOK TIME: APPROXIMATELY 3-4 HOURS

1 piece fresh pork belly (4–5 pound [2–2.25 kg]), skin on

3 tbsp (20 g) fennel seeds

2 tbsp (10 g) crushed red pepper flakes

1 tbsp (7 g) black peppercorn

2 tbsp (5 g) minced fresh sage

1 tbsp (3 g) minced fresh rosemary

3 garlic cloves, minced

Kosher salt

1 pork tenderloin (1–1½ pound [455–680 g]), trimmed

½ orange, peeled, seeded, thinly sliced

Butcher's twine
4 good sized chunks of apple wood and hickory (or oak) 2 pieces each

Put the pork belly skin-side down; arrange loin in the center. Roll belly around the loin so the short ends of the belly meet. If any of the belly or loin overhangs, trim the meat (save for another time). Unroll and set the loin aside.

Toast the fennel seeds, red pepper flakes and peppercorns in a small skillet over medium heat until fragrant, about 1 minute. Transfer spices into a bowl and let them cool. Grind spices to a medium grind in a spice mill, and transfer them to a small bowl, along with the sage, rosemary and garlic. Set the mixture aside.

To assemble, set the pork belly skin-side down. Using a knife, score the belly flesh in a checkerboard pattern ⅓ inch (8 millimeters) deep so roast will cook evenly. Flip the belly skin-side up. Using a paring knife, poke a lot of ⅛ inch-deep (3 millimeters) holes ½ inch (13 millimeters) apart throughout skin all over the belly. Don't be afraid, you want to poke a lot of holes in it; this will help to crisp up the outer skin.

Using the jagged edge of a meat mallet, pound the skin all over for 3 minutes to tenderize. This will help make the skin crispy when roasted.

Turn the belly and generously salt both the loin and the belly; rub both with the fennel mixture. Arrange the loin down the middle of the belly. Top it with orange slices. Roll the belly around the loin; tie crosswise with butcher's twine at ½ inch (13 millimeter) intervals. Transfer roast to a wire rack set in a rimmed baking sheet.

Refrigerate roast, uncovered, for 1 day to allow skin to air-dry; pat occasionally with paper towels.

Let the porchetta sit at room temperature for 1–2 hours. Season the outside of the porchetta with kosher salt and cracked black pepper.

(continued)

PORCHETTA (CONTINUED)

➤ Preparing the spice mixture

➤ Slicing the orange

➤ Applying the spice mixture

➤ Rolling porchetta

PORCHETTA (CONTINUED)

You'll be setting up your WSM for low and slow cooking (about 250°F [121°C]), then finishing it off hot and fast so you can get that outside skin nice and crispy! For the first part of the cook, fill the water pan about three-quarters full with hot water. You will be removing the water from the pan on the second half of the cook. Just before putting the porchetta roast on the WSM, you can add the wood chunks.

Place the porchetta on the top grate and cook until an instant-read thermometer inserted into center of meat registers 145°F (63°C). At this point remove the middle section of the WSM, remove the water pan, dump water and place the pan back in. Throw in a full chimney of lit charcoal, wait about 10 minutes, reassemble the WSM and adjust it for a temp of about 350°F (177°C). Continue cooking until an internal temperature of about 160°F (71°C). If the skin is not yet deep brown and crisp, remove the water pan and place the porchetta onto the bottom grate and roast for 10 minutes more. Let rest for 30 minutes. Using a serrated knife, slice into ½-inch (13-millimeter) rounds.

➻ Continue to roll porchetta

➻ Searing outside of porchetta

BEEF SHORT RIBS

If you've never had beef short ribs before, you're missing out on one of life's great pleasures. Beef short ribs are the most flavorful and tender pieces of meat on a bone you can imagine. And really, if you make them right, the handy little stick it comes on is only incidental—the meat will fall off the bone if you so much as breathe on it.

YIELD: 4 SERVINGS ★ COOK TIME: APPROXIMATELY 4½ HOURS

16 ounces (475 ml) dark American larger
1½ cups (355 ml) beef stock
4 pounds (2 kg) bone-in beef short ribs

1 onion, rough chopped
4 cloves garlic, coarsely chopped
Olive oil
Salt and pepper
Chili powder

Dutch oven with cover
3–4 chunks of hickory or oak

For this recipe you'll want to set the WSM for low and slow cooking (approximately 225–250°F [107–121°C) for the first part then set it up for high heat for the braising. While the WSM is heating up, apply some olive oil to the inside of the Dutch oven and place it on the bottom rack. This will allow the Dutch oven to heat up, as well as catch all the dripping from smoking the short ribs. More flavor!!

Mix beer and beef stock together to make the braising liquid.

Season the short ribs with olive oil, salt, pepper and chili powder. Place the short ribs on the top rack and smoke for about 2 hours. (About 15 minutes before they are done smoking, fire up a full chimney of lump charcoal.)

Remove short ribs and add to the heated-up Dutch oven, meat side down. Add the onions, garlic and braising liquid (about three-quarters of the way covered), cover and put back onto the WSM. (Here is were you will disassemble the WSM, remove the water from the pan and put back empty and add about a full chimney of lit charcoal (you can use lump charcoal at this point because it will burn a little hotter than regular briquettes). Reassemble the WSM.

Cook for an additional 2–2½ hours at approximately 325–350°F (163–177°C), or until tender. You know they are tender if you can probe them and it feels like the probe is going into soft butter. Remove and let rest for about 15 minutes, then serve.

➳ **Beef short ribs are different than beef ribs. Traditional beef ribs are taken from the cow's rib cage and are long. Short ribs are beef ribs that have been taken from the plate cut.**

DIJON GARLIC HALF CHICKENS

This is a simple recipe; it's so juicy, tender and totally packed with flavor. The brine is what helps make this chicken so tender and juicy and that tang from Dijon mustard really brings this dish together.

YIELD: 6–8 SERVINGS ★ COOK TIME: APPROXIMATELY 2 HOURS

---

2 whole chickens
Chicken Brine (page 69)
¼ cup (65 g) Dijon mustard
¼ cup (60 ml) olive oil
¼ cup (40 g) minced garlic
2 tbsp (5 g) fresh parsley, chopped
2 tbsp (30 ml) honey
2 tbsp (30 ml) lemon juice
1 tbsp (15 g) sea salt

3–4 chunks of apple wood

Set up your WSM for low and slow cooking, about 250°F (121°C). Fill the water pan halfway with hot water, and put your smoke wood in about 5 minutes before putting the chicken on. You will start cooking using the low and slow method. Later on, you will set the cooker up for high heat to finish the chicken.

In a bowl, combine the mustard, olive oil, garlic, parsley, honey and lemon juice. Set it aside.

Remove and throw away the bag of chicken parts. Place the whole chicken breast-side down on a large cutting board. Find the spine of the chicken. Using a boning knife or a sharp chef's knife, cut the length of the chicken on each side of the spine and remove it. Open the chicken up still breast-side down. Find the keel bone. Using your knife, score the chicken on either side of the keel bone. Grab the large end and with a front to back rocking motion, remove it by hand and discard it along with the spine. Slice the length of the chicken between each breast. Remove any unwanted fat and extra skin.

Place the chicken halves into the brine, and put it in the fridge for about 4 hours—you can go up to 12 hours if you want.

Remove from brine and rinse off and pat dry with paper towels. Take your seasoning mixture and rub it all over both chickens. Peel back the skin of the breasts and rub it directly on the meat. Replace the skin. Now take your sea salt and sprinkle it evenly over all four chicken halves. Let this sit for about 15 minutes.

Place the chicken halves on the top grate skin-side up. Cook at 250°F (121°C). After an hour of cooking, start to check the temperature. When the internal temperature reaches 145°F (63°C) start to light a full chimney. When you see flames shooting out of the top of the chimney, it's ready to dump in the cooker. Remove the entire center section of the WSM; keeping the cover on, dump the lit chimney on and let sit for 5 minutes. During that time, carefully remove the water pan from the WSM, dump water and return pan to the smoker. Place the middle section back on the base. Adjust the bottom vents to be fully open. This will help maintain a higher cooking temperature—you want about 350°F (177°C). Cook for another 15 minutes—this will finish cooking the chicken and crisp up the skin with the water pan removed. (When cooking your chicken, check to make sure the internal temperature is at least 165°F [74°C].)

LAMB SHANK—SMOKED AND BRAISED

Lamb shanks are not very tender and require a long cooking time to help break down all that tough meat. You know the old saying, "Good things come to those who wait?" Well, this is one of those good things, and it's certainly worth the wait. The slight smoke flavor and richness of this dish will have your friends and family talking about how you are the next big cooking sensation.

YIELD: 6 SERVINGS ★ COOK TIME: APPROXIMATELY 4–5 HOURS

6 lamb shanks (about 1½ pounds [680 g] each)

Olive oil

Salt and pepper

Garlic powder

4 tbsp (60 g) butter

2 onions, chopped

3 large carrots, cut into ¼" (6 mm) round pieces

10 cloves garlic, minced

2 tbsp (20 g) flour or cornstarch

1 (28 ounce [795 g]) can whole peeled tomatoes

1½ cups (355 ml) chicken stock

1½ cups (355 ml) beef stock

2 cups (475 ml) red wine, full bodied like a cabernet

1½ tbsp (4 g) fresh rosemary, chopped

2 tsp (4 g) fresh thyme, chopped

Dutch oven with cover

4 chunks of apple wood

Set up the WSM for slow and slow cooking (approximately 250°F [121°C]) for the first half of the cooking process, with the water pan filled halfway. Then you'll be setting it up for high heat (approximately 350°F [177°C]) to finish it, with no water in the water pan. Just as you're putting the lamb on the WSM, add the wood chunks.

Coat the lamb shanks in olive oil and season with salt, pepper and garlic powder. Place lamb shanks onto the top grate of the WSM, cook for about 2 hours.

An hour into the cook, prepare the Dutch oven for the second half of the cooking process.

An hour and forty-five minutes into the cook, fire up a full chimney of charcoal for high heat cooking.

At a stovetop, over medium heat, add the butter, onions, carrots and garlic and sauté until onions are translucent, about 5 minutes. Stir in the flour or cornstarch and continue cooking for another 3 minutes. Add in the tomatoes, chicken stock, beef stock and red wine and simmer for about 10 minutes. Next, add the rosemary and thyme, and season with salt and pepper to taste. Simmer for another 10 minutes, remove from heat, cover and set aside until the shanks come off the WSM. Remove the shanks from the WSM and place them into the Dutch oven. If you don't have a cover, use HD aluminum foil as a lid.

Remove center section of the WSM and dump water pan. Add the full chimney of lit charcoal, and wait about 5 minutes for the coals to catch. Reassemble the WSM and place the Dutch oven on the bottom rack. Continue cooking for another 2–3 hours or until you reach an internal temperature of 180°F (82°C).

Remove from the WSM, put shanks on a platter, cover with foil and let rest for about 15–20 minutes. Over medium-high heat, boil the liquid in the Dutch oven to thicken for about 15 minutes.

Serve the shanks over mashed potatoes or creamy polenta and spoon the thickened sauce over them. Enjoy!!

LEG OF LAMB

Lamb is one of those meats you either love or hate. I love lamb! I love the slightly earthy, gamey taste it has, and when prepared and cooked right, it's one of the best meats around. I have served this lamb recipe to my family a few times during Easter, and they always tell me I better serve it again the following year! So, I guess they really love this dish.

YIELD: ABOUT 8-12 SERVINGS ★ COOK TIME: APPROXIMATELY 2-3 HOURS

1 bone in leg of lamb (6–7 pounds [2.75–3 kg])

LAMB MARINADE
¼ cup (60 ml) honey
2 tbsp (30 g) whole grain mustard
2 tbsp (5 g) fresh rosemary, chopped
1 tsp (5 g) course ground pepper
1 tsp (2 g) lemon zest
Juice of 1 lemon
3 cloves garlic, minced
2 tbsp (30 g) kosher salt
2 tbsp (7 g) coarse black pepper
2 tsp (3 g) garlic powder

4 hickory wood chunks
2½ gallon (9.5 L) zippered storage bag

Heat your WSM for low and slow cooking, about 250°F (121°C). Fill the water pan halfway with hot water, and add the smoke wood when you put the meat on the cooker. Later on in the cook, you are going to remove the middle section and put the cooking grate directly over the coals. This will sear the meat at the end of the cook and create a crispy exterior.

Mix ingredients for the marinade in a bowl. Place the lamb into a 2½-gallon (9.5-liter) zippered storage bag and pour the marinade over the leg of lamb. Marinate it in the refrigerator overnight; be sure to turn it over a few times to ensure even flavor distribution.

Place the leg of lamb on the top grate, and cook until the internal temperature is about 130°F (55°C) for medium rare or to 140°F (60°C) for medium, about 2–3 hours.

With a pair of heat-resistant gloves, remove the center section, and without spilling the water from the water pan, carefully set it aside, leaving the cover of the WSM on.

Carefully stir up the coals and let them get nice and hot, about 10–15 minutes.

Remove the top grate with the lamb and put it directly over the coals. Sear the meat for about 2–3 minutes per side.

Remove meat from the cooker, and loosely tent with foil. Allow it a rest time of about 15–20 minutes before carving.

BEEF TENDERLOIN

The beef tenderloin is the gold standard of beef cuts. It's tender, versatile and pretty easy to cook. It's a very lean piece of meat that has a mild flavor to it because it does not contain a lot of fat. With a little bit of trimming and some seasoning, beef tenderloin will transform into the perfect holiday meal.

YIELD: ABOUT 8 SERVINGS ★ COOK TIME: APPROXIMATELY 1 HOUR AND 20 MINUTES

1 whole beef tenderloin (5–6 pounds [2.25–2.75 kg])

WET RUB

¼ cup (60 ml) olive oil
2 tbsp (5 g) flat leaf parsley, chopped finely
1 tsp (5 g) kosher salt
2 tsp (5 g) black pepper
2 garlic cloves, minced
1 tsp (3 g) chili powder

HORSERADISH WHOLE GRAIN MUSTARD SAUCE

3 tbsp (50 g) Dijon mustard
3 tbsp (50 g) whole grain mustard
½ cup (60 g) sour cream
¼ cup (55 g) mayonnaise
¼ cup (60 g) prepared extra hot horseradish

Plastic wrap
Butcher's twine
2–3 chunks apple wood

Heat your WSM for low and slow cooking, about 250°F (121°C). Fill the water pan halfway with hot water, and add the smoke wood when you put the meat on cooker. Later on in the cook, you are going to remove the middle section and put the cooking grate directly over the coals to sear the meat at the end of the cook to finish.

In a small bowl, mix all of the wet rub ingredients and put aside until ready to use. Then, mix all the mustard sauce ingredients together and store in the fridge until ready.

Next, you want to trim the beef tenderloin; it's going to save you about half the money to buy the tenderloin untrimmed. It only takes about 15–20 minutes to trim it yourself. It's pretty easy and straight forward. You will need a sharp boning knife for this. Remove the meat from the packaging and pat dry with paper towels.

Pull off as much of the loose fat and membrane as possible with your fingers from both sides of the tenderloin. Remove the "chain;" this is a length of muscle and fat attached to one side of the tenderloin. It will come off in a single piece and can be pulled off by hand, but you may want to use a knife to assist with this. Trim any areas of fat or membrane that have been exposed from removing the chain.

On the butt end, carefully remove the pockets of fat in the two creases on either side of the tenderloin, making sure to remove as little meat as possible. Remove the silver skin. This is a length of white/silver connective tissue that runs the whole length of the tenderloin. You want to make sure you remove it; it's not very pleasant to eat. Starting in the middle, take the tip of the knife and pierce under the edge of the silver skin, then angling the blade slightly up towards the skin in a sawing motion, cut until you reach the end of the skin. Angling the blade up helps you to remove the skin without losing very much meat. Continue this until all the silver skin is removed. Continue to trim and remove any areas of extra fat.

(continued)

BEEF TENDERLOIN (CONTINUED)

➜ Searing the tenderloin

➜ Slicing the tenderloin

Tie the tenderloin up with the butcher's string. Tying it up will help the tenderloin to cook evenly throughout. On the small end of the tenderloin, you want to take about 2 inches (5 centimeters) of the tail and flip it under towards the center of the tenderloin; take about two pieces of string and tie it up to secure it. Next, you want to tie up the butt end; you can use 3–4 pieces of string for this. Then tie up the middle, again using 3–4 pieces of string.

Once the tenderloin is trimmed and tied up, apply the seasoning rub all over to work into the meat and wrap in plastic wrap. Let it sit for about an hour. Remove plastic wrap.

Place the tenderloin onto the top grate of the WSM, and cook until an internal temp of 120–125°F (49–52°C) for rare/medium rare or 130–135°F (55–57°C) medium rare/medium. This will probably take about an hour cooking at 250°F (121°C).

With a pair of heat resistant gloves, remove the center section. Without spilling the water from the water pan, carefully set it aside, leaving the cover of the WSM on. Carefully stir up the coals and let them get nice and hot, about 10–15 minutes. Remove the top grate with the tenderloin and put it directly over the coals and sear meat for about 2–3 minutes per side.

Remove and let rest for about 10–15 minutes. Slice and serve with the whole grain mustard/horseradish sauce.

PRIME RIB ROAST

Growing up, my family always had turkey at Thanksgiving and Christmas. Naturally, the turkey was often dry and overcooked. As an adult, I started cooking prime rib for some holidays instead. When it is done right, it is simply out of this world. I like my prime rib cooked to medium rare (warm red center). With this recipe you will be able to achieve that goal at the next family gathering!

YIELD: 8-10 SERVINGS ★ COOK TIME: 3-4 HOURS

---

1 rib eye roast bone-in (10–12 pounds [4.5–5.5 kg])

Olive oil

Salt and pepper

Granulated garlic

First thing you're going to want to do is rub the entire roast down with some olive oil. Next, season aggressively with the salt, pepper and garlic. This will be some of the tastiest bark you will ever eat! Leave it on the counter covered with some plastic wrap for about an hour.

While you are waiting for the roast to get to room temperature, go ahead and get your WSM ready to fire up. For this you are going to use one full chimney of lit coals and will be cooking on the middle rack, with no water pan for the first 30 minutes. Dump the chimney into the base of the WSM (all three vents should be wide open). Go ahead and assemble the WSM (leave the water pan out) and put the middle rack in. You're looking for a temperature of about 400–425°F (205–218°C) at the lid.

Place the roast on the rack bone-side up for about 20 minutes. This will help form that flavorful crust I mentioned earlier. After 20 minutes, remove the roast and let it rest. Remove the center section of the WSM, and add about two chimneys of unlit charcoal. Wait about 5 minutes and assemble the WSM, close all three vents to about 25 percent open and put the water pan in full of water. Place the top grate on and put the roast on top of the grate bone-side down. You will be looking for a temperature of around 225°F (107°C). Cook until the meat reaches an internal temperature of 125°F (52°C). Remove roast, wrap in it foil and in a couple of old towels and place in an empty cooler. Let it rest for about 1½ hours.

➼ **Note: You will want to have your butcher remove the meat from the bone and then have him/her tie it back up with butchers string. Trust me it will save you time on the back-end when slicing.**

CHAPTER FOUR

THE SECRETS TO GRILLING/HIGH HEAT ON THE [WSM] AND OTHER SMOKERS

One of the most outstanding features of the WSM is its versatility. With some simple repositioning of its existing parts, you can convert the WSM for use as a standard grill. The key to grilling is to obtain a very high temperature (400°F [205°C] and higher) and cook your food close to the heat source. To accomplish this on the WSM, remove the charcoal rack and charcoal ring from the base of the cooker and place them on the middle cooking rack. When repositioning the lower rack, make sure you rotate it so that the two cooking grates are running perpendicular to each other. You can leave the water pan in place (but if you do, line it with foil to protect it from ashes).

Light a full chimney of lump charcoal (remember, lump charcoal burns hotter than briquettes, so it is better suited for this type of cooking). When flames are shooting over the top of the chimney, dump the charcoal into the ring. Refill the chimney half full with unlit charcoal and carefully spread the contents over the lit coals. Using tongs, stack the charcoal in a pile on one side of ring. Stacking the charcoal creates two cooking zones: a hot zone and a cool zone. Use the hot zone, located directly above the charcoal, to sear meats when they first go on the grill. Use the cool zone, which has no charcoal beneath it, to finish cooking the seared meat. Make sure that the three bottom vents are wide open to maximize airflow.

Let the charcoal burn for a few more minutes (the cooking temperature should reach about 450°F [232°C]). Sear the meat with the lid on the WSM. Searing with the lid on assists in eliminating flare ups and helps prevent the meat from burning. After you sear both sides, move the meat from the hot zone to the cool zone and let it finish cooking. Place the lid on the WSM when cooking in the cool zone.

GARY'S POPPERS

These poppers are the perfect little appetizers for your next cookout or party. Our friend Gary makes these all the time. They are pretty easy to make and they are always delicious. I personally think it's the pickled jalapeño that makes this dish so amazing. Well, the bacon helps too. Everything is better with bacon, right?

YIELD: ABOUT 32 POPPERS ★ COOK TIME: 20 MINUTES

1 pound (455 g) sirloin tip strips
Lawry's Seasoned Salt
½ tsp pepper
1 pound (455 g) bacon
6 ounces (170 g) cream cheese
4 ounces (114 g) sliced pickled jalapeños
1 tbsp (15 ml) olive oil

Cut the steak into 1 inch (2.5 centimeter) pieces, and season with seasoned salt, pepper and olive oil. Refrigerate for 1 hour to overnight.

Set up your WSM for two-stage grilling.

Cut each piece of bacon into three pieces. Lay out each piece of bacon, and place the steak strip at one end. Apply about a teaspoon (5 grams) of cream cheese, place one or two jalapeño sliced on top of cream cheese and roll bacon around tightly. Secure with a toothpick.

You can cook these in about 3 separate batches. Place the poppers over direct heat and sear for about 1–2 minutes per side, then remove to the cooler side of the WSM and continue to cook indirectly for about 15 minutes. Repeat for the remaining poppers.

➳ Two-stage grilling is when you have a hot section (all the hot coals to one side of the grill) to sear the meat and a cool section (where there are no coals) to finish cooking the meat indirectly.

GRILLED ROMAINE LETTUCE

The first time I ever had this dish was a at a friend's restaurant. I saw it on the menu and thought, no way, but decided to try it anyway!! Let me tell you, I fell in love and I now look for it every time we go out to eat! Romaine lettuce has some natural sugars inside that are not released by smothering it with salad dressing. They are only released when grilling the lettuce. Combine that with something as simple as grated cheese and the results are wonderful.

YIELD: 4 SERVINGS ★ COOK TIME: 5 MINUTES

BALSAMIC VINAIGRETTE
½ cup (120 ml) olive oil
¼ cup (60 ml) good balsamic vinegar
2 tbsp (30 ml) agave
½ tsp fresh cracked pepper

2 heads romaine lettuce, washed and cut in half
Olive oil
Salt and pepper to taste
½ cup (50 g) freshly grated Parmesan cheese

First, mix all the vinaigrette ingredients and store in the fridge until ready to use.

Fire up the WSM for cooking like a grill, one zone, (page 161).

Take the 4 halves of romaine and lightly drizzle olive oil on the cut side, sprinkle with salt and pepper.

Place them onto the WSM—this should only take about 1–2 minutes, so you want to be checking the under side, and you are looking for a nice char. Flip and do the same for the other side.

Remove from the WSM and take the Parmesan cheese and sprinkle over each half (cut side) and drizzle with balsamic vinaigrette.

A way to serve this is when the lettuce comes off the WSM, you can chop it up, put it in a bowl and toss with the cheese and balsamic dressing.

GRILLED CORN ON THE COB

Grilled corn on the cob is an easy-to-make item that is very popular at all of our cookouts and summer-time parties. It is not only tasty, it never fails to impress your guests. Fresh corn on the cob can be grilled on the WSM in its own husks. In the husk makes for a more dramatic presentation! Grilled corn is especially delicious when you add herbs and spices to the ear of the corn before grilling it. The herbs and spices liven up the flavors and add an interesting spin on basic roasted corn. It's easy to do—just use your favorite variety of corn!

YIELD: 6 SERVINGS ★ COOK TIME: 20 MINUTES

---

6 fresh ears of corn
Olive oil
Butter
Salt and pepper

If the ears of corn have many layers of husk on them, peel off only the first couple of layers, leaving a few layers for protection. Do not remove all the layers.

Begin by pulling the husks of the corn back (but do not completely remove them). Remove and discard only the silk.

Soak the whole cobs in a pot of cold water for up to 60 minutes. Be sure the ears are completely covered with water. This will provide extra moisture for cooking and will steam the corn kernels inside the husks.

While the corn is soaking, fire up the WSM for grilling two-stage cooking (see note on page 162). After soaking, remove the corn from the water and shake off any excess water.

Brush the kernels with olive oil or butter. Note: I've used olive oil instead of butter. I think butter is best applied after the corn comes off the grill, just before you eat it.

If desired, before you re-wrap the corn in the husks, add a little garlic, chopped onion, nutmeg, salt and black pepper. For an international twist, try using herbs such as basil, cilantro or oregano. Then reposition the husks back over the kernels and tie each ear with a piece of loose husk or twine.

Place the prepared ears of corn onto the WSM, rotating the corn as needed to keep it from getting charred too much on one side. After a couple of turns, place the corn on indirect heat and close the cover. Allow the corn to slowly continue cooking for approximately 15–30 minutes.

Remove the corn from the grill. Be careful and wear oven mitts, as the corn will be very hot! Grasping one end with an oven mitt or dish towel, peel the husks and remaining silk from the top down (like a banana)—they should all come off in one piece. Ashes will get on the corn, but this is ok. Rinse the corn under warm running water to remove any excess ash and silk. Serve with butter and enjoy!

SAUSAGE GRAVY AND BISCUITS

Every time I go south of the Mason Dixon line I have to eat sausage gravy and biscuits for breakfast each morning. This has to be the all-time greatest comfort food to have for breakfast. I love the richness and creaminess of the sausage gravy, and soaking up all that great flavor with a nice soft and flaky biscuit.

YIELD: 6 SERVINGS ★ COOK TIME: 30 MINUTES

1 pound (455 g) breakfast sausage (regular or spicy)

½ tsp fresh ground black pepper

1 shallot, finely diced

6 tbsp (50 g) flour

3 cups (710 ml) whole milk (not that low fat stuff)

Salt to taste if needed

4 warmed biscuits cut in half (page 100)

1 cast iron skillet

Set up your WSM for cooking like a grill. Set it up so you have the hot coal piled on one side of the WSM, where all the cooking will be done.

Cook the sausage in a large cast iron skillet for 8–10 minutes or until thoroughly cooked, stirring frequently. Drain and reserving drippings; place the sausage in a bowl. Return half of the drippings to the skillet.

Add shallots and fresh ground pepper and cook for about 3 minutes. Add flour and remaining drippings to the skillet; stir with a wire whisk until well blended. Cook for 6–8 minutes or until browned, stirring constantly. Gradually stir in your milk; cook and stir for 3–5 minutes or until mixture thickens and comes to a boil.

Add the sausage, and cook for 1–2 minutes or until thoroughly heated, stirring frequently. Serve over biscuits.

SHRIMP TACOS WITH LIME SLAW

My teamate Alan took this recipe down to Memphis in May 2011, where it took first place in the seafood catagory. If you really want to impress your friends and family at your next cookout, then look no further. After they eat these shrimp tacos, they'll be asking what restaurant made them—it's that good!

YIELD: 8 TACOS ★ COOK TIME: 5 MINUTES

---

2 pounds (910 g) uncooked shrimp (16–20 shrimp per pound) peeled and de-veined

Smokin' Hoggz Dry Rub (page 23)

8 (6-inch [15 cm]) corn tortillas (flour tortillas are OK too)

¼ cup (30 g) sour cream

2 tbsp (30 g) mayonnaise

Grated zest from 1 lime

Juice from 1 lime

1 (16 ounce [450 g]) package coleslaw mix

2 scallions (green onion), diced

1 jalapeño, seeded and diced

2 tbsp (5 g) fresh cilantro

Salt and pepper to taste

1 large tomato, seeded and diced

12 ounces (340 g) sweet chili sauce

Canola oil

Set up your WSM to cook like a grill for direct heat cooking.

In a bowl, combine sour cream, mayonnaise, ½ lime zest and lime juice. Add coleslaw mix, green onions, jalapeño and cilantro and mix well. Season with salt and pepper and stir in the tomato. Keep this in the refrigerator until ready to use.

In a bowl, toss the shrimp with oil, the rest of the lime zest, salt and pepper and let sit for about 30 minutes. I find it easier to put the shrimp on skewers after this and season with the dry rub. Cook the shrimp for about 2–3 minutes per side over direct heat. Then toss the shrimp in the sweet chili sauce.

Grill tortillas over direct heat for about 1 minute per side.

To assemble the tacos, spoon the slaw mix into the bottom of the tortilla, top with 3–4 shrimp and enjoy!!

PORK TENDERLOIN STUFFED WITH BACON JAM

Pork tenderloin is the filet mignon of pork. It's a very lean piece of meat and can dry out very quickly when overcooked, so it needs to be cooked quickly over high heat. This is a simple recipe with some great flavor!

YIELD: 3 SERVINGS ★ COOK TIME: 18 MINUTES

---

1 pork tender loin (1½ pounds [680 g])
Smokin' Hoggz All-Purpose Rub (page 35)
½ cup (120 g) Bacon Jam (page 172)
1 cup (240 g) Apple BBQ Sauce (page 173)

Butcher's twine

Set up the WSM for grilling using the two-zone cooking method.

Take the tenderloin and butterfly it open. To do this, take a sharp knife and cut lengthwise along the whole tenderloin, making sure you don't cut through the back side. Open it up so it lays flat. Season the inside with rub and add the bacon jam, close it up and use the butcher's string to secure it closed, about 1 inch (2.5 centimeters) apart. Season the outside of the tenderloin with more rub.

Place the tenderloin directly over the coals and put the cover on. Cook for about 7 minutes. Flip the tenderloin and do the same thing for the other side—do not place it back on the same spot, place it on another hot spot. (The reason why you don't want to put it back in the same spot is the place where the meat was has cooled down and you want all the heat you can get, on a fresh new spot). This will allow you to get some nice grill marks—cook for another 6 minutes. Now, take the tenderloin and move it to the other side of the WSM where there are no hot coals, and continue cooking for another 5 minutes. When the internal temperature reaches 145–150°F (63–66°C), it's done!

Remove from heat and let rest for about 10 minutes. Slice into ½ inch (13 millimeter) pieces and serve with Apple BBQ Sauce.

BACON JAM

This sweet little condiment is a fantastic addition to include at holiday parties or your occasional weekend breakfast at home.

YIELD: ABOUT 1½ CUPS (180 G) ★ **COOK TIME: 3-4 HOURS**

1½ pounds (680 g) sliced bacon, cut cross-wise into 1" (2.5 cm) pieces
2 medium yellow onions, diced small
3 garlic cloves, smashed and peeled
½ cup (120 ml) cider vinegar
½ cup (100 g) packed dark-brown sugar
¼ cup (60 ml) pure maple syrup
¾ cup (180 ml) brewed coffee

Set up the WSM to cook like a grill, two-zone cooking (page 162).

In a large cast iron skillet, cook the bacon, stirring occasionally, until fat is rendered and bacon is lightly browned, about 20 minutes. You may need to move the pan to the cooler side to avoid burning the bacon. With a slotted spoon, transfer bacon to paper towels to drain. Pour off all but 1 tablespoon (10 grams) of the fat from the skillet (reserve for another use); add onions and garlic, and cook until onions are translucent, about 6 minutes. Add vinegar, brown sugar, maple syrup and coffee and bring to a boil, stirring and scraping up browned bits from skillet with a wooden spoon, about 2 minutes. Add the bacon and stir to combine.

Now set up your WSM for high heat cooking (approximately 300–325°F [150–160°C]).

Keep the mixture in the cast iron skillet and cook uncovered, until the liquid is syrupy, 3½–4 hours. Transfer the mixture to a food processor; pulse until coarsely chopped. Let it cool, then refrigerate in airtight containers, up to 4 weeks.

APPLE BBQ SAUCE

Apple and pork go together like peanut butter and jelly, so the next time you're looking to jazz things up a bit, try making some of this apple BBQ sauce. Trust me, you're gonna love it.

YIELD: ABOUT 3 CUPS (360 G) ★ COOK TIME: 20 MINUTES

---

1 cup (200 g) packed brown sugar

½ cup (130 g) applesauce

½ cup (160 g) apple butter

½ cup (120 g) ketchup

¼ cup (60 ml) lemon juice

½ tsp kosher salt

½ tsp coarse black pepper

1 tsp (1 g) paprika

½ tsp garlic powder

½ tsp cinnamon

¼ tsp allspice

Combine all of the ingredients in a saucepan, and cook over medium heat until the sugar is dissolved. Cool and store in an airtight container in the fridge until ready to use.

BLUE RIBBON PORK CHOP

This pork chop recipe was one of the first recipes we did in which we got a first place call. Unbeknownst to me, the judges fondly referred to them as "lollipop chops." I still have judges coming up to me and saying they still have never had a pork chop cooked as perfectly as they did that day!

YIELD: 4 SERVINGS ★ COOK TIME: 20–25 MINUTES

4 double-bone pork chops at least 2"
(5 cm) thick with clean bones (Frenched—
have your butcher do it)
1 bottle Lawry's Steak and Chop Marinade
Smokin' Hoggz Dry Rub (page 23)
1 cup (320 g) apple butter
½ cup (120 ml) apple juice

Set up your WSM for grilling. With this set up you'll want to have the coals on one side for direct heat and have nothing on the other side for indirect heat to finish the chops.

Place pork chops into a zippered plastic bag and add marinade. Marinate for at least 4 hours to overnight; remove chops and season with dry rub.

Cook over high heat 5 minutes each side then move to cooler side, and cook until an internal temperature of 145–150°F (63-66°C) for medium-rare, longer if you like it more well done.

Baste with apple butter/juice mix.

LAMB CHOPS WITH PEPPER JELLY

When I think of lamb chops, for some reason I always think of special occasions like an anniversary or a special event worth celebrating. This is a great recipe for two people. My wife is a very picky eater, but surprisingly she really likes lamb! And she really likes this recipe. I like to surprise her with these lamb chops every once and while. You can serve this with your favorite side dishes.

YIELD: 2 SERVINGS ★ COOK TIME: 10 MINUTES

DRY RUB

2 tbsp (15 g) chili powder

1 tbsp (6 g) ground cumin

2 tsp (4 g) allspice

2 tsp (8 g) white organic sugar

2 tsp (10 g) salt

1 tsp (3 g) white pepper

1 tsp (3 g) black pepper

4 double-bone lamb chops

1 cup (160 g) pepper jelly

2 tbsp (30 g) whole grain mustard

2 tbsp (30 ml) champagne vinegar

1 handful of apple wood chips

Set up your WSM for cooking like a grill with two-zone cooking, one for searing the meat and the other for finishing the meat. Sprinkle the apple wood chips over the hot coals just before searing the meat.

Mix the rub ingredients together and sprinkle the dry rub on each chop, being sure to evenly cover both sides. Cook over high heat. Grill the steaks for 1½ minutes per side.

Move the chops over to the cool side, and finish cooking until the chops reach an internal temperature of 150°F (66°C).

In a saucepan, heat up the pepper jelly, mustard and vinegar just enough to incorporate the ingredients.

Remove the chops from the grate and let them rest (about 5 minutes), while the chops are resting, spoon the sauce over each chop.

STRIP STEAK WITH HORSERADISH SAUCE AND CARAMELIZED ONIONS

Better than restaurant quality, that's what this recipe is all about. A perfectly cooked, well-seasoned New York strip steak, topped with a little horseradish sauce and some beautiful golden caramelized onions—now that's my kind of steak!

YIELD: 4 SERVINGS ★ COOK TIME: 30 MINUTES

HORSERADISH SAUCE
1½ cups (180 g) sour cream
½ cup (120 g) prepared white horseradish
6 tbsp (20 g) fresh chives diced
4 tsp (20 ml) fresh lemon juice

4 (16 ounce [455 g]) strip steaks (about 1½" [4 cm] thick)
Salt, pepper and olive oil
1 stick of unsalted butter
1 small sweet onion thinly sliced

Whisk all of the horseradish sauce ingredients to blend in a small bowl. Season with salt and pepper. Cover and chill. This can be made 2 days ahead of time.

Melt the butter in a large skillet over medium heat until it starts to foam. Add the onions and reduce the heat to low. Cook, stirring occasionally, until the onions are a dark amber but not burned, about 30 minutes. Season with salt and pepper. (You can make it up to 1 week ahead and store in the fridge. Bring the onions to room temperature before serving.)

Set up your WSM to cook like a grill, making sure you have a hot zone for searing the steak and a cool zone for finishing the steaks. Rub the steaks down with olive oil. Liberally season both sides of the steaks with salt and pepper. Let the steaks sit out for about 45–60 minutes before you put them on the WSM.

Grill the steaks for about 3 minutes per side (if you want to get those awesome grill marks, turn the steak about a quarter turn after about 1½ minutes). Move the steaks over to the cool side, finish cooking until rare (120°F [49°C]), medium-rare (125°F [52°C]) or medium (130°F [55°C]). This will depend on the thickness of the steaks. Remove and let rest for about 5 minutes. Serve with onions on top and sauce on the side.

RIB EYE STEAK WITH HERBED TRUFFLE BUTTER

I love rib eye steak! My favorite part of the rib eye is the tail. The tail is from the outer part of the steak, and it has a piece of fat that separates it from the rest of the steak. To me it has the most flavor, and it is always tender. I usually eat the other part of the steak and save the tail as a little treat for the end of my meal.

YIELD: 4 SERVINGS ★ COOK TIME: 15 MINUTES

TRUFFLE BUTTER
1 pound (455 g) unsalted butter, room temperature
White truffle oil to taste
Kosher salt to taste
¼ cup (10 g) fresh chopped parsley

BEEF RUB
2 tbsp (30 g) kosher salt
2 tbsp (15 g) pepper
1 tsp (3 g) granulated garlic
2 tsp (7 g) chili powder

4 (16 ounce [455 g]) boneless rib eyes
¼ cup (60 ml) olive oil

In a small mixing bowl, combine the parsley butter and truffle oil together. Season with salt to taste. On a large piece of plastic wrap, place the butter/truffle mixture and form into a log, about 1 inch (2.5 centimeters) thick. Wrap the log tightly. Refrigerate overnight.

Set up your WSM to cook like a grill, making sure you have a hot zone for searing the steak and a cool zone for finishing the steaks.

Combine all of the beef rub ingredients and put them into a shaker bottle. Rub the steaks down with the olive oil. Liberally season both sides of the steaks with the rub. Let the steaks sit out for about 45–60 minutes before you put them on the WSM.

Grill the steaks for about 3 minutes per side (if you want to get those awesome grill marks, turn the steaks about a ¼ turn after about 1½ minutes). Move the steaks over to the cool side; at this point you can add 2 slices of the truffle butter to each steak. The butter will melt down over the steaks and soak in all that awesome flavor. Finish cooking until medium-rare (125°F [52°C]). This will depend on the thickness of the steaks. Remove the steaks and lest them rest for about 5–10 minutes before serving.

PIZZA

I love pizza. Now, you might be thinking that a round, oven-baked flat bread dish, layered with tomato sauce, cheese and a few other toppings, seems out of place in a barbecue cookbook. You might be thinking it, but you're wrong. You can actually cook pizza on the WSM, and I'll teach you how!

There are so many different styles of pizza to choose from: Chicago thick pan, Neapolitan, New York thin crust and even oddball square-shaped pizzas. The variety of flavor combination you can use on pizza is simply amazing. I think that I could eat pizza for every meal, every day, for the rest of my life, and still not get bored of this dish!

WORKFLOW

Configure the WSM for pizza.

If you were to cook pizza using a uniform layer of hot charcoal, the center of the pizza will burn. To prevent this, I recommend spreading out the hot charcoal in a circle. The circle of hot charcoal should dip in the center, producing less heat in the middle and more heat at the outer edge.

After you arrange the hot charcoals in the WSM, put the top cooking rack in place. When you put the top cooking rack in place, make sure you also place your pizza stone on the rack! You must let the pizza stone heat up slowly. If you do not, and you expose the stone directly to high heat, the stone might crack.

Wait for the WSM to obtain a temperature of 450°F (232°C). This usually takes about 20 minutes. While you wait for the WSM to heat up, roll out the pizza dough. You can make your own dough, or purchase dough (which speeds up the cooking process). I recommend making a pizza that is 14 to 16 inches (36 to 41 centimeters) in diameter. Place the dough on the pizza stone, and let it cook for 2 to 3 minutes. Flip the dough, and let it cook for 2 more minutes. Remove the dough from the pizza stone, and then add the pizza toppings.

PULLED PORK PIZZA

This recipe is one of my favorites, not only because I love pulled pork but it's also a great way to use up any leftover pulled pork you have. This recipe has won us many awards in grilling competitions through the past couple of years.

YIELD: SERVES 4 ★ COOK TIME: 15 MINUTES

1–1½ cups (240–360 ml) BBQ Sauce (page 23)
1 pizza dough ball
1 pound (455 g) pulled pork
1 cup (115 g) white cheddar cheese
1 cup (115 g) Monterey Jack cheese
¼ cup red onion or green onions (scallions), finely diced

Take about half the BBQ sauce and spread it on the dough, add the pulled pork and cover it with both cheeses. Now you can add either type of onion you want. Put the pizza in the WSM; after about 5 minutes, check to see if it's done (cheese should be nice and melted). The bottom of the crust should be golden brown; check the bottom of pizza by lifting it with a spatula or a pizza peel. Cut and serve.

BACON, PEAR BLUE CHEESE

I was inspired to do this pizza when my teammate Alan and I were out having a couple of beers and spotted a version of this pizza on the menu. We really enjoyed it, so I knew I had to find a way to recreate it. Here is my version of a fantastic pizza from some time ago. If you're looking for a pizza with a nice mix of flavors, look no further.

YIELD: SERVES 4 ★ COOK TIME: 15 MINUTES

½ cup (125 g) blue cheese dressing
1 pound (455 g) bacon or pancetta, diced
½ cup (70 g) crumbled blue cheese
1 cup (115 g) white cheddar cheese
2 pears, diced
1 cup (40 g) arugula
¼ cup (60 ml) good balsamic vinegar
Whole wheat dough

Spread the blue cheese on and add the bacon or pancetta. Sprinkle on the crumbled blue cheese. Next, add the diced pears and the white cheddar cheese. Put the pizza in the WSM, and check pizza after about 5 minutes. It's done when the cheese is melted and the bottom of the crust is golden brown. Remove the pizza and add the arugula and drizzle with balsamic, cut and serve.

COO COO JUICE

I had to include at least one drink in with this book. I mean, what's a summer BBQ without a little adult beverage, right? After all, you have to have something to do while you're waiting for the food to cook. This drink is a Smokin' Hoggz tradition at most of the contests we compete at, especially in the summer time. Enjoy and drink responsibly!

YIELD: ABOUT 24 (8-OUNCE [240-ML]) SERVINGS

---

1 (1.75 liter) bottle of mango rum (or any flavored rum)

1 gallon (4 L) strawberry, orange, banana Crystal Light

5 pound (2 kg) bag of ice cubes

2 gallon (8 L) capacity drink cooler

16 ounce (475 ml) red Solo cups

Pour about half of the ice into the drink cooler and add the rest of the ingredients. Stir until well mixed. Fill each cup with ice and add the coo coo juice. Relax and enjoy!!

ABOUT THE AUTHORS

BILL GILLESPIE is the founder and Head Pit Master for the World Champion Smokin' Hoggz BBQ team. Bill spends his days working for the local utility company as a Design Engineer, but his true passion is grilling and cooking BBQ. For over 25 years Bill has been perfecting his craft in BBQ cooking in his back yard for friends and family. In 2005 Bill joined the BBQ circuit and in 2008 formed Smokin' Hoggz BBQ. Since then he has gone on to win multiple Grand Championships and numerous awards including the 2011 Jack Daniel's World BBQ Championship, the most prestigious BBQ competition on the circuit.

TIM O'KEEFE has lifetime membership in the Kansas City Barbeque Society (KCBS), the largest organization in competition barbecue. Based out of the Boston area, his love of barbecue once inspired a cross-country road trip to Lockhart, Texas, just to eat brisket! Stops in Kansas City, Missouri; Gulfport, Mississippi and Memphis, Tennessee, helped round out his understanding of regional variations in this unique American cuisine. A certified barbecue judge, Tim has judged nearly 30 contests sanctioned by KCBS. Tim has a master's degree in writing from Northeastern University and has contributed articles for *National Barbecue News*. He blogs about competition barbecue at fromthejudgestable.com.

ACKNOWLEDGMENTS

To my family for always believing in me and teaching me to always stay true to myself and to look at life for the positives.

My wife, Shaune Gillespie for giving me inspiration and encouragement.

My teammate and right-hand man (and sometimes left) Alan Burke, for keeping me calm and focused when I needed to be.

Chris Hart for teaching and giving me the tools I needed to make championship BBQ.

Tim O'Keefe for taking all my chicken scratches and ideas and transforming them into real words people can understand.

Ken Goodman for his incredible vision in making the food look amazing.

To my publisher, Will Kiester, my editor, Marissa Giambelluca and the entire staff at Page Street Publishing for giving me the opportunity to do this book and helping me along the way.

Eric and Cindy Mitchell for taking time out of their busy schedule to help out with the photo shoot.

Chad and Nicole Humphrey for taking the leap and believing in me from the very beginning.

To all my BBQ friends for being so freakin' awesome.

INDEX